coming Home

A SEASONAL GUIDE TO CREATING FAMILY TRADITIONS

Rosanna Bowles

Photographs by John Granen

STEWART, TABORI & CHANG ⁓ NEW YORK

dedication

To my Mother, my muse, who taught us the importance of family and traditions.
You showed us how love is expressed by establishing rituals of caring. To my Father,
a savvy New Yorker who opened our world to new and exciting experiences.
Also to my dear family, who has shown me unconditional love and supported me
in every endeavor.

Published in 2010 by Stewart, Tabori & Chang
An imprint of ABRAMS

Text copyright © 2010 by Rosanna Bowles
Photographs copyright © 2010 by John Granen, except the photograph on page 109, which is ©2010
Henderson Shorter

Library of Congress Cataloging-in-Publication Data
Bowles, Rosanna.
  Coming home : a seasonal guide to creating family traditions / Rosanna Bowles ;
  photographs by John Granen.
  p. cm.
  ISBN 978-1-58479-836-1
  1. Home economics. I. Title.
  TX145.B588 2010
  640--dc22

                              2009035981

EDITOR: Jennifer Levesque
DESIGNER: Glenn Gontha | gonthadesign.com
PRODUCTION MANAGER: Tina Cameron

The text of this book was composed in Dear Sarah Pro, Today Sans, and Vista Sans Alternate.

Printed and bound in China
10 9 8 7 6 5 4 3 2 1

Stewart, Tabori & Chang books are available at special discounts when purchased in quantity for
premiums and promotions as well as fundraising or educational use. Special editions can also be created
to specification. For details, contact specialsales@abramsbooks.com or the address below.

ABRAMS
THE ART OF BOOKS SINCE 1949

115 West 18th Street
New York, NY 10011
www.abramsbooks.com

6 Introduction

9 Spring
31 Spring Recipes

51 Summer
87 Summer Recipes

99 Fall
125 Fall Recipes

145 Winter
163 Winter Recipes

180 Acknowledgments
182 Index

contents

introduction

When I was growing up, our family life revolved around traditions and rituals passed down through the generations. The values my sisters and I learned were based on life lessons that our parents, grandparents, and neighborhood friends learned during their lives. We were fortunate to be raised in a community with many teachers: individuals who helped us navigate the challenges of growing up, getting married, and becoming mothers.

The foundation on which we built our lives was based in the life lessons that these wise and caring people taught us. Unfortunately, this communal support and sense of tradition have all but disappeared from today's world.

Families are scattered across the globe, neighbors no longer take a vested interest in the well-being of one another, and rituals and tradition are widely considered perfunctory obligations to perform without love, enthusiasm, or care, and they often lack any sort of real meaning. Our everyday customs no longer hold the warmth of human connection.

But I want to change that.

In writing this book, I have eagerly complied the recipes, experiences, and life lessons that highlight the beauty and significance of tradition and ritual. I wrote this book as a guide, in the hopes that it will help others recapture and reestablish these soulful life experiences that have faded from our world.

In the course of my career, I have built a business that creates products that encourage interaction over the breaking of bread and for celebrations honoring small, special moments in life such as a child's birthday, a national holiday, or even just a cup of afternoon tea with a neighbor. These are the rituals that infuse our lives with richness and create invaluable human connections.

We face an array of daunting challenges. But by staying focused on the things that are truly important—family, friends, and the care of the hearth and home—we can guarantee ourselves a happy, fulfilling life.

My hope is that this book will encourage you to incorporate the notion of simple pleasures into your daily lives. By capturing and appreciating the beauty that can be found wherever we look, we can take pleasure in life's small moments of happiness. Enjoy . . . and come home. It's where everything good begins.

Roanna

spring

Spring is a

season of "becoming."

The earth is ready for renewal, and new life bursts forth. The arrival of spring is nature's way of reminding us that exhilarating changes are under way and that we are lucky participants in this transformation.

Change is, quite literally, in the air as the fresh breezes of the season blow in through newly open windows. Along with the changes in the weather, spring brings a beautiful, chaotic frenzy of growth and physical transformation. The air is sweeter, trees are in blossom, and a green patina of fresh growth covers the earth. The symbols of rebirth are all around. Dormant plant life begins to come alive again. New babies are born. All of this life makes spring the ideal season to break out of old patterns. This is the time to change old habits and start new ones, to throw tired old ways out and look forward to new possibilities of personal growth. The arrival of a new season encourages us to embark on new adventures.

Spring offers us what we all long for: hope. No matter what our age, the adage "Hope springs eternal" is relevant.

Effect a Change in Your Environment

Plant new flowers or greenery around your home. If you have a garden, position potted plants where you can easily see them from the windows, so you can enjoy them whether you're inside or out. Nurture the new plants and enjoy watching them change with new foliage and blossoming flowers. Because of the care you give plants as they grow, watching a plant flourish can be surprisingly satisfying. If you don't have a garden, buy potted plants that can live indoors. Having something green and alive in the room adds a wonderful hint of nature to an interior.

Update the colors in your home. Paint a wall with a fresh new color that reflects the change in the weather. This is an inexpensive and dramatic way to redecorate a room. Even easier is to move the furniture around or take away furniture to unclutter your living space. Clear the way to create a feeling of airiness. This simple exercise opens up a space and imparts a sense of freshness and change appropriate to the season.

Update your table linens and home accessories to reflect the change in season. Use soft colors and muted pastels. Go through your cupboard and change your dish and table settings. Be creative. Mix and match different patterns. Add assorted floral patterns for a spring garden look. If you're a fan of solid colors, set a table with multiple colors of mismatched dishes. Pull out the "nice" porcelain dishes and use them for everyday meals, pairing them with simple place mats and clean stainless-steel flatware for a casual table setting. Beautiful porcelain should not be stowed away for occasional use. Porcelain brightens a table and changes the mood of even the most routine dining experience.

Fill the house with freshly cut flowers. Many grocery stores offer fresh-cut flowers at a reasonable price. Tulips and daffodils are usually the first flowers of spring. Buy several bunches and place them in a large-mouth vase. The fresh burst of color from the flowers instantly enlivens a living space. Put a tall, oversized white vase filled with pussy willows or forsythia, or clippings from fruit trees like cherry and apple (which, if you're lucky, you can gather from your yard or a friendly neighbor's), in the center of your dining table, in the entryway, or on a sideboard or any other large service area. Smash the ends of the stems with a hammer to help the branches absorb water. Remember that flowers make people happy, so put them in any room you use regularly.

Play spring-themed music that you know the lyrics to and sing along. I like the soundtracks to *Mamma Mia!* and *The Sound of Music* for this purpose. It may seem a bit hokey, but singing—even tone-deaf singing—is a wonderful mood lifter, and everyone can use a bit of joyful silliness every now and then. Sing loudly, even if you're off key.

When you eat "in season" and the vegetables are locally grown, you'll find such a delightful difference in taste and texture from out-of-season supermarket varieties.

Savor Spring Vegetables

As the warming weather reveals beautiful new elements in the world, the earth also yields wonderful treats just waiting to be eaten: spring vegetables. The season for each spring vegetable is short lived, so take advantage of the selection available at your local farmers' markets—snap up the best of the season as soon as they appear, because they may be gone the next week. Some my favorite early spring vegetables include asparagus, artichokes, and baby English peas. All three can be incorporated into salads or a springtime pasta dish. When you eat "in season" and the vegetables are locally grown, you'll find such a delightful difference in taste and texture from out-of-season supermarket varieties. Once you've tried eating in season, you'll never go back. The recipes at the end of this chapter make good use of spring vegetables and also include accompanying dishes to make a complete seasonal meal.

In spring, with the house full of fresh flowers and pretty pastel decorations, I'm inspired to cook easy, light meals that feature top-quality vegetables and excellent traditional spring meats. I enjoy putting together one-dish pasta dinners using the fresh ingredients my family and I have been missing for months, and bright, crisp green salads with tangy dressings. I also make a point of preparing the herbed pork roast that's a common feature of special spring dinners in Italy. (SEE RECIPES, PAGE 31.)

For dessert I draw on my mother's legacy and make several spring desserts that have become family favorites: Butterscotch Pie, Coconut Cream Pie, and Cindy's Bunny Cake, named for my older sister (SEE PAGES 42, 43, AND 45). These recipes originated in the 1950s and 1960s, but I've updated and lightened them, taking into consideration today's taste trends and health concerns. These three recipes give you a variety of options for the tone you want to set with your dessert: The butterscotch pie is simple, rich, and comforting, the coconut is fresh and sophisticated, and the bunny cake is both decorative and very tasty, with a frosting coated with delicious shaved coconut.

Get Outside and Play

Spring offers us a variety of ways to change our old habits. Lightening our cuisine and eating more vegetables and less meat can be very satisfying—as well as an opportunity to lose any extra weight we may have put on during the winter months.

As the weather changes, it also means we're able to spend much more time outside—walking, exercising, and simply playing. Taking a short half-hour walk around your neighborhood is a great way to take note of nature's beauty. Another way to take advantage of the weather with your family is to play the outdoor games from your childhood—structured ones like softball or capture the flag, or more casual activities like kick the can or throwing a Frisbee. Doing something fun outdoors is quality time that also helps you stay in shape.

As the days lengthen, it's fun to incorporate games into an early evening on a weekday or a quiet Sunday afternoon. It's a lovely way to feel young again and pass on the notion of free play to our children.

Throw a Children's Spring Birthday Party

My older daughter Alessandra's birthday is in May, and my younger daughter, Francesca, has a birthday that falls right after Christmas. Because the holidays are such a hectic time, I always throw Francesca's birthday party in March. Although it's still officially winter, I try to put a spring twist to the theme to transform the environment into a fun, colorful, light celebration that contrasts with the lavish decorations and extravagant mood of the winter holidays.

This year, for Francesca's twelfth birthday, I re-created a party from my own childhood. I chose color combinations that were popular in the '60s, and we made posters and decorations reflective of the era. Vases of hot pink gerbera daisies filled the house, trays piled high with homemade cupcakes graced the table, and in the background played the music from *Across the Universe*. Her guests even played vintage Barbie, a board game from my childhood. I also invited the mothers of Francesca's friends for a pre party glass of Champagne. I served homemade stove-top popcorn along with pizza and a variety of organic "junk food." We watched Francesca and her friends on what was probably the last year of their official "girlhood" and sang Francesca "Happy Birthday". Then the girls headed downstairs with sleeping bags in tow, ready to enjoy their first independent sleepover.

Planning a Child's Party

Over the past twenty years that I've thrown birthday parties for my daughters, I've learned some important lessons for how to make a birthday party successful.

1. Pick a theme. We chose the 1960s because we love the colors and design elements of the era. It's often easier to come up with fun foods, decorating ideas, and party activities when you have a framework in which to brainstorm.

2. Design a fun invitation on the computer or craft handmade invitations that define the party. Let people know that this is an event to look forward to!

3. Play a variety of age appropriate games; the most popular at my daughter's twelfth birthday party was the vintage Barbie game, and we also rented movies like *Big, Mamma Mia!, The Parent Trap,* and *Grease.*

4. Provide food that's easy to deal with and at least somewhat healthy. To accomplish these goals, I ordered pizza from a restaurant that uses fresh, local ingredients, and I made my own cupcakes from a good boxed mix that had no preservatives and additives. I made big bowls of homemade popcorn and served fun snacks like Smart Puffs and Hava Corn Chips from San Francisco (another throwback from the theme era), and for an indulgent treat, I set out bowls of colorful M&Ms. (SEE RECIPES, PAGE 49.)

5. Set up a space that takes into account the interests of your child and his or her friends. For the sleepover in our basement, I piled up lots of blankets and set out big puffy floor pillows and beanbag chairs for easy movie viewing and late-night chats.

Revisit Childhood Pleasures

During my childhood, outdoor games were the mainstay of free play and yielded endless hours of entertainment. Growing up in the '50s and '60s or '70s, unsupervised outdoor play was the best thing about spring.

My favorite outdoor games included softball, kick the can, hide and go seek, red light green light, and kickball. With just a few changes, we can enjoy some of these bygone games today. Instead of leaving your child alone all day, which really isn't possible in today's world, join your children on the weekend and teach them these fun games. Invite your child's friends to your own backyard or visit a city park together. For children and adults alike, playing games is a pleasure. Try to encourage your child to do as many activities as possible that are based on creativity and free play.

Taking a short half-hour walk around your neighborhood is a great way to take note of nature's beauty.

Dance

The dramatic changes that come as winter gives way to spring make our bodies and souls want to express the joy of this new environment. One activity that makes the most of this newfound energy is dancing. Music and dance can temper any mood, elevate the spirit, and release a rush of endorphins. The sense of well-being that comes from dancing is a priceless gift that we experience far too infrequently. Music and dance release tension, allowing our souls to become free. Choose any music that moves you. After thirty minutes of dancing and listening to some great music, a transformation of spirit will have taken place. You will *feel* good.

Disco artists that make you want to boogie all night:

Barry White
The Bee Gees
Donna Summer
Sly and the Family Stone
The Village People
KC and the Sunshine Band

Oldies that make you want to sing and dance:

Burt Bacharach, *The Best of Burt Bacharach*
The Beatles, *Abbey Road*
Marvin Gaye, *Let's Get It On*
Al Green, *Al Green's Greatest Hits*
James Brown, "I Got You (I Feel Good)"

World music that takes you to another place:

Various Artists, *The Soul of Cape Verde* (Cape Verde)
Bebel Gilberto, *Momento* (Brazil)
Astrud Gilberto, *The Girl from Ipanema* (Brazil)
Laurindo Almeida and Charlie Byrd, *Tango* (Argentina)

Music to help you pretend you can dance like a principal in a Broadway musical:

West Side Story soundtrack
Mamma Mia! soundtrack (film version)

For an escape to a European environment without leaving home, play this:

The Umbrellas of Cherbourg soundtrack
Amélie soundtrack
A Man and a Woman soundtrack

Spring Cleaning

Spring cleaning has been a part of human history for thousands of years, and it is often integrated into the religious practice of cleansing the home prior to a spring festival. In North America, spring cleaning took place when March arrived and the weather got warm enough to open the windows and let in the fresh air without the worry of summer insects invading the home. The sweet spring winds would carry the dust out of the house and refresh the heart of the home. Of course, thorough cleaning need not be done only in the spring; it's just that the warmer weather encourages us to fling open the windows and purge old dirt that has accumulated from a long winter of indoor living, and we're enthusiastic about cleaning so it gets done faster and the process is more pleasant overall.

Spring cleaning can seem daunting when you think of cleaning an entire home top to bottom, but if you break the process down into small projects—perhaps concentrating on bathrooms one day, bedrooms the next, and so on—spring cleaning is not only manageable but easy. To help you get going, put on your favorite music while you clean. For my mother, this meant Frank Sinatra every Saturday morning.

A Spring Cleaning Plan

1. Kitchen

Clean the refrigerator, removing all of the food and wiping down the shelves, walls, and bins with a nontoxic cleaner. Throw out old items and rearrange the food by type: dairy on one shelf, condiments in the door shelves, lettuces and fresh herbs in the crisper drawer, and other vegetables and fruits in a second drawer if you have one. Put food that should be used quickly in an easy-to-see and easy-to-access spot. Store leftovers in glass and porcelain containers. To further minimize the use of plastic products, use upside-down plates to cover bowls containing leftover food.

2. Bathrooms

Go through the medicine cabinets and throw away all medicine that's old and/or past the expiration date. To prevent excess chemicals from entering the sewage system, don't flush the medicine down the toilet. To dispose of pills, crush them in a container and cover them with water. Fill the container with kitty litter to absorb the water containing the chemicals. Transfer to a plastic bag, seal, and put in the trash. Clean the toilet: Use a brush for the inside of the toilet, then wipe down the outside with environmentally friendly cleaners. Clean the sinks and shower (and look for any signs of mold). Clean the entire floor, paying special attention to the area around the toilet bowl.

3. Bedrooms

Go through your closets and ask your family to do the same to theirs. Remove clothes you haven't worn for a couple of seasons. Put them aside and donate them to a local charity or clothing bank. Clean the floors, including under the beds where the dust collects. Open the windows while vacuuming to let the dust out. Europeans habitually air out their bedding and pillows by hanging them over the edge of the window to get rid of dust or mites. Do this regularly when the weather is nice.

4. Dining room and family room

These areas will collect the most dirt due to frequent use. Take all the cushions off the chairs and couches and vacuum under the cushions. You'll be amazed at the amount of dust and crumbs you'll find. Move the furniture, and you'll discover that more dust awaits you. Vacuum thoroughly under the dining room table. If you have an area rug, remove it and clean under it. Take the rug outside and put it over a railing, where you can beat the dust out and then let the rug air for an afternoon.

Decorate for Spring

Now that the house is spotless, or as close to spotless as you want it to be, freshen up your rooms with springtime decorations. Each spring festival has its own set of symbols we can use to decorate our homes, but in general I decorate my home with green boughs, branches, potted spring flowers, and all the symbols of rebirth: bunnies, eggs, chicks, and ducks.

In your garden, find a nicely shaped barren branch or a spring branch with budding flowers. To preserve freshness, smash the bottom of the branch with a hammer so it will better absorb water. Place the branches in a tall vase of water. Decorate the branch with tiny symbols of the season: blow out eggshells and tie them with a ribbon, tie skinny pastel ribbons in bows with long tails, and set tiny figurines of bunnies, chicks, or ducks amid the twigs. Display in a hallway or on a mantle for a striking spring statement.

Find a hand-hewn willow basket about five and a half inches (14 centimeters) high. Line it with plastic and set small, colorful spring plants still in their containers inside the basket. Between the containers, put moss from a floral-supply store or home-décor store. This makes a charming centerpiece on a dining room table or as a beautiful explosion of color anywhere in the home. Be sure to water it regularly, misting the moss occasionally to revive its bright green color.

Find unusual vessels like 1960s Danish modern coffee pots or tall heavy cut crystal vases and fill them with branches or pussy willows.

Fill old silver-plate trays that are about ten inches (25 centimeters) long and about three inches (7.5 centimeters) deep with faux moss or grass. Nestle some pale-colored faux eggs in the moss and place the trays around the house.

Find some fun, vintage-looking bunnies, eggs, or birds and create a small tableau on an old silver tray. Pair with votives or a dramatic pair of candlesticks to center the scene. Place in a prominent spot such as on a sideboard, the center of the dining table, or on a kitchen island.

Celebrate Spring Festivals and Holidays

In the springtime, joy is bursting out all over. The arrival of spring has always involved festivals that manifest the collective sigh of relief we experience when winter finally ends and the weather becomes pleasant. The rites of spring span many cultures, offering us lots of opportunities to celebrate the new season.

Some of the most well-known spring holidays include Easter, Passover, and May Day. Some lesser-known holidays include the vernal equinox, the Buddhist New Year, and St. George's Feast, which is celebrated in Great Britain. Many of these festivities include extensive use of fresh greenery as decoration, and symbols of birth such as lambs and bunnies, a celebration of the first new blooming of nature.

Whether marked by a favorite recipe or a ritual from decades past, spring customs are an important part of bringing family and friends together. Children love to partake in traditions that reflect their family's history. Share old stories from past generations. Although they may be more than half a century old, these stories are often still relevant to our lives today. My children love the stories about how their grandmother celebrated spring holidays during the Great Depression and World War II, as well as stories about those same holidays from my childhood.

May Day is one of my favorite holidays. In most parts of the country, May is when spring becomes truly apparent, with blossoming fruit trees and bulbs bursting forth in a blaze of color. These heady days of truly warm weather give us all spring fever, a feeling of joy that we naturally want to celebrate.

People throughout the Western world celebrate May Day, and the holiday has a long history harking back to medieval times. When I was a little girl, my mother showed me how to make May baskets from construction paper and took me to fill them with flowers from our garden. Then we would sneak over to our neighbors' homes, drop the baskets on their doorsteps, ring the doorbells, and run away. When our friends opened the door, a charming handmade basket filled with flowers greeted them.

The gesture of celebrating spring by giving a gift of nature is a wonderful tradition that unites us as a community, encouraging us to give of ourselves while cultivating an awareness of the gifts that nature has to offer. My children love participating in the May Day custom, as do the other neighborhood children who live near us. I have one young neighbor, now seventeen years old, who has been ringing my doorbell on May 1 since she was six years old. Every year I'm touched by her sweet gesture and thoughtful heart.

Go on a Spring Break Vacation

The tradition of university spring break began in the early 1920s when East Coast American colleges decided that students needed a break from the rigors of the stringent academic schedule. To recuperate from a winter of intense study and prepare for a few months' more work before classes let out for the summer, students would go to health spas or the seaside. The tradition has since evolved into a rite of passage, and Ft. Lauderdale, Florida, has become the headquarters for a weeklong celebration of freedom from studies with a taste of liberation and unending parties.

However, spring break can mean a variety of things for students of all ages. The break presents the opportunity to get some sun after slogging through a long winter or to reunite as a family in a place where you love to relax. When I was a child we didn't go to exotic places but stayed close to home and spent a week at the Oregon coast. The weather wasn't great, but we made up for it by cooking and eating fresh fish from the Pacific Ocean,

playing board games, and catching up on our pleasure reading. For us, spring break was a special time— a time to be together as a family. We took long walks along the vast shoreline, hunted for shells, and had hot-dog roasts on the beach, with s'mores for dessert. Simplifying a family holiday by stripping away the glitz associated with an exotic destination can allow you to instead focus on being together in the moment. These less-glamorous memories will be just as vibrant later in life.

Planning Your Next Spring Break Vacation

1. Find a place to go that's close to home. Locate state parks, historic locations, and places of great beauty that are nearby.

2. Find a house to rent, if possible: it will be more comfortable than a hotel and may end up being less expensive if your stay is more than a few days. Look for a house in a setting that encourages outdoor activities you can all enjoy together, like hiking, fishing, biking, swimming, or picnicking. Look for a rental with a kitchen so you can easily prepare family meals together.

3. Invite grandparents, aunts, uncles, and cousins along. Far too often, we omit our extended families due to emotional and physical distances. Remember how important an extended family is to a healthy, happy nuclear family unit. The richness of multiple generations is a great asset to the family core.

4. Finally, choose a place where you know you'll be able to relax and enjoy a few supremely lazy days. It's a rare treat in today's world to have periods of unplanned, unfilled time in which our minds are free to wander.

spring recipes

Asparagus in the Oven

This is a quick and delicious seasonal dish that can add a touch of the Mediterranean to any meal. Asparagus is a versatile vegetable that can be served in a variety of different ways, but one of my favorites is to roast the asparagus in the oven with a drizzle of extra-virgin olive oil, a hint of garlic, and a sprinkling of sea salt. The asparagus becomes slightly caramelized and crunchy.

Many dishes go well with roasted asparagus, the obvious choices being roast chicken, pork roast, or pork chops (SEE RECIPES, PAGES 41, AND 39). For a less conventional, vegetarian pairing, try an omelet with fresh parsley, chives, and a mild soft cheese, or even scrambled eggs with herbs accompanied by crusty buttered toast.

SERVES 4

Extra-virgin olive oil

1 clove garlic, smashed

1 pound (454 g) asparagus, ends trimmed

Sea salt

Preheat the oven to 350°F (177°C) (Gas mark 4).

Lightly drizzle the bottom of a roasting pan with oil. Rub the pan with the garlic clove. Arrange the asparagus in a single layer in the pan. Season with salt to taste and drizzle lightly with more oil. Roast for 20 to 25 minutes, until slightly caramelized.

Asparagus with Fried Eggs

This is a very simple dish that can be on the table in about 15 minutes. The fresh green crunch of asparagus and the softness of creamy egg create a lovely and satisfying eating experience. I dust the egg and asparagus with grated Parmigiano-Reggiano cheese and a grinding of sea salt. It is a delicious and easy meal to prepare. Serve with a light white wine like Pinot Grigio.

SERVES 2

4 tablespoons (60 ml) extra-virgin olive oil

2 pounds (908 g) very fine asparagus, stalked with ends trimmed

4 large organic free-range eggs

2 tablespoons (12 g) freshly grated Parmigiano-Reggiano cheese

Sea salt and freshly ground black pepper

In each of two large sauté pans, heat 2 tablespoon (30 ml) of the oil over medium-high heat. Divide the asparagus between the two pans and sauté until just tender, about 10 minutes. Crack the eggs over the asparagus, 2 in each pan. Cook until the yolks are cooked to the desired degree of doneness. Sprinkle evenly with the cheese and season with salt and pepper to taste. With an oversized spatula, carefully transfer the eggs and asparagus to serving plates. Serve immediately.

Frittata di Asparagi
(Asparagus Frittata)

A frittata is an endlessly adaptable Italian baked omelet and a staple of *la cucina povera*, "the poor kitchen"—or more accurately "the simple kitchen"—in which leftovers are never wasted but rather turned into gastronomic delicacies. Use any fresh vegetables that happen to be in season, and lightly sauté them in extra-virgin olive oil with a little garlic and onion before adding them to the eggs. You can also use leftover cooked vegetables. Here I top the frittata with mozzarella and Parmigiano-Reggiano, but you can use any cheese you have on hand. Experiment with adding small bits of cured meats like prosciutto or pancetta. Try this as a main course; it is delicious with a simple salad, crusty bread, and a nice red table wine.

SERVES 4

¼ cup (60 ml) extra-virgin olive oil

½ pound (227 g) asparagus, ends trimmed, chopped

½ cup (75 g) shelled baby English peas (or frozen baby peas)

1 clove garlic, minced

3 scallions, white parts only, minced

12 leaves baby spinach, chopped

6 large eggs, beaten

¼ cup (25 g) freshly grated Parmigiano-Reggiano cheese

¼ cup (25 g) freshly grated mozzarella cheese

Sea salt and freshly ground black pepper

2 tablespoons (10 g) chopped fresh parsley

Preheat the oven to 350°F (177°C) (Gas mark 4).

In a medium sauté pan, heat half of the oil over medium-high heat. Add the asparagus, peas, garlic, scallions, and spinach and sauté until just tender, 10 to 15 minutes. Set aside.

Coat the bottom of an ovenproof sauté pan with the remaining oil and heat on the stove-top over medium heat. Add about half of the eggs. Let the eggs cook to form a layer, and then move the cooked layer with a spatula to allow the uncooked egg to flow to the bottom. Add the sautéed vegetables. Sprinkle the cheeses over the vegetables, then cover the cheese with the remaining eggs, and the parsley. Season with salt and pepper to taste.

Bake for 10 to 15 minutes, until the egg is firm. Remove from the oven, cut into wedges, and serve immediately.

Artichokes

Every spring, I look forward to the fresh crop of artichokes that hits the markets starting in March. It's an unusual vegetable, and some may find its spiny appearance intimidating, but it's so easy to prepare and so rewarding—especially when you get to the toothsome, flavorful heart—that it will likely become a regular feature of your spring menus as well. A special bonus that the artichoke offers is healthfulness: One large artichoke has only 25 calories, no fat, and 170 milligrams of potassium, and it is an excellent source of vitamin C. Artichokes also contain folate, magnesium, and lots of dietary fiber.

SERVES 4

4 large California globe artichokes

Juice of 2 lemons

1 clove garlic, smashed, plus 2 cloves minced

6 tablespoons (¾ stick) (84 g) good-quality salted butter

Wash the artichokes under cold water. Cut off the stems at the base and remove any small leaves. Fill a large pot with 2 to 3 inches (5 to 7.5 cm) of water. Add half of the lemon juice and the 1 smashed garlic clove. Bring to a boil. Place the artichokes upright in the pot. Cover and cook at a low boil for 35 to 45 minutes, until the artichoke's base can be pierced with a fork or you can easily pull off a leaf. Drain the artichokes upside down.

In a small saucepan, heat the butter, minced garlic, and the remaining lemon juice. When the butter is melted, pour it into individual ramekins. Serve the artichokes with the lemon butter as a dipping sauce. Tell your guests to pull one leaf at a time from the artichoke and dip it in the sauce, then scrape the leaf with their teeth to pull off the tender inner flesh of the artichoke. After the large outer leaves are all eaten, paper-thin leaves remain. These can be pulled out in sections and eaten, but the best part of an artichoke is the heart. After you've eaten all of the leaves, remove the hairy choke with a tablespoon until you reach the heart. Dip the heart in the butter sauce, and enjoy.

California Brown Rice

This rice is deliciously nutty, with lots of flavor and texture, and works beautifully alongside simply prepared vegetables and roast pork. It's a very healthful whole grain that's grown in America.

SERVES 6

1 cup (192 g) California brown rice

1 cup (250 ml) chicken broth, preferably Swanson's organic

1 tablespoon (14 g) butter

In a small saucepan, combine the rice and broth. Bring to a full boil. Turn the heat to the lowest setting and cover the pan. Simmer for 30 to 45 minutes (do not remove the lid before 30 minutes is up), until the rice is tender and all the liquid has been absorbed, then remove from the heat. Add the butter and stir gently until it has melted. Let the rice stand, covered, for about 10 minutes, then serve.

Insalata Mista (Mixed Salad)

I like this refreshing salad because it cleanses the palate and lightens the meal. It's also visually appealing due to the different shades of green accented by the bright orange of the carrot. I always buy local romaine, because it actually tastes like lettuce rather than a watered-down version of the real thing. Enjoy this salad alongside any pasta dish or with any type of meat or fish.

SERVES 6

1 head romaine lettuce

½ pound (227 g) arugula

1 carrot, coarsely grated

¼ cup (60 ml) extra-virgin olive oil

1 teaspoon (5 ml) balsamic vinegar or red wine vinegar, plus more to taste

Sea salt and freshly ground black pepper

Wash the romaine and cut off the bottoms of the leaves. Cut into 2-inch (5 cm) lengths. Place the lettuce in a bowl of water and rinse by swishing the cut lettuce. Spin dry in a salad spinner and place in a large salad bowl. Set aside.

Rinse and clean the arugula the same way. Chop off any large stems that aren't tender. Put it in the bowl with the romaine.

Add the carrot. If you're not serving the salad right away, soak two paper towels with water, ring them out, and spread them out over the bowl; refrigerate until ready to serve. (This is a trick I learned from my mother. It works like a charm to keep the salad fresh and crisp until you dress it.)

When ready to serve, drizzle the salad with the oil and vinegar; start with 1 teaspoon (5 ml) vinegar and add more to taste. Season to taste with salt and pepper and toss with salad tongs. Serve immediately.

Small Roasted Red Potatoes

This is a wonderful side dish to serve with any meat. The undersides of the potatoes become a crunchy golden brown, and the tops are soft and tender. Because they're small, these potatoes satisfy the need for a starch without being too heavy and overwhelming.

SERVES 4

¼ cup (60 ml) extra-virgin olive oil

1 pound (454 g) small red potatoes

Sea salt

Preheat the oven to 350°F (177°C) (Gas mark 4).

Coat the bottom of a small, heavy porcelain or enamel roasting pan with the oil. Cut the potatoes in half and place them cut side down in the pan. Sprinkle with sea salt to taste. Bake for 20 to 45 minutes (depending on the size of the potatoes). Halfway through the baking, flip the potatoes over so the cut side is exposed. Bake until tender when pierced with a fork and golden and crunchy on the cut side. Use a spatula to remove the potatoes from the pan and serve immediately.

Pasta Ortolano (Greengrocer-Style Pasta)

Pasta Ortolano is the quintessential spring pasta, using the best of the fresh produce available in early spring. It is inspired by my love of the Italian countryside and the bounty of vegetables available. The dish offers a delightful mixture of textures: velvety wilted spinach, slightly crisp asparagus, and firm spring peas that burst upon the tongue. The flavors are light and distinctly green. This is a very fresh-tasting dish that is easy to eat and makes you feel very healthy after you eat it. Serve with Prosecco, a sparkling white wine from Italy.

SERVES 4

¼ cup (60 ml) extra-virgin olive oil, plus more if necessary

4 ounces (113 g) spinach, washed and chopped into 3-inch (7.5 cm) pieces

1 pound (454 g) very thin asparagus, ends trimmed, cut into 2-inch (5 cm) lengths

½ cup (75 g) shelled spring peas or frozen baby peas

1 clove garlic, minced

Sea salt

¼ cup (60 ml) dry white wine

1 pound (454 g) dried penne rigate pasta, preferably De Cecco brand

Parmigiano-Reggiano cheese, in one piece for grating

In a large sauté pan, heat the oil over medium-high heat. Add the spinach, asparagus, peas, garlic, and 1 teaspoon (6 g) salt and sauté, stirring constantly, until the spinach is wilted and the asparagus and peas are tender but not mushy, 10 to 15 minutes. Add the wine and cook until it has almost evaporated, about 5 minutes.

Meanwhile, cook the pasta in a large pot of boiling salted water until al dente (with a little give), 12 to 15 minutes. Drain in a colander.

Put half of the vegetable mixture in the pasta pot, then return the pasta to the pot and top with the remaining vegetable mixture. Toss to combine the pasta and vegetables, adding salt to taste if necessary. Add a drizzle of oil if the sauce seems too dry. Grate cheese over the top and serve immediately.

Paglia e Fieno (Straw and Hay Pasta)

This dish got its name because the mixture of spinach linguine and plain linguine looks like a mound of straw and hay when served. I first ate this dish in Italy when I was a student spending my junior year abroad, and it became a favorite of mine the moment I tasted the saltiness of the prosciutto against the creamy texture of the sauce and the sweet explosion of the fresh peas. This is a perfect dish to serve in the spring as soon as fresh peas are available. Serve family-style in a large, low bowl, with a mixed green salad (SEE RECIPE, PAGE 35) and the rest of the Pinot Grigio.

SERVES 4

⅓ cup (75 ml) extra-virgin olive oil

2 to 3 tablespoons (28 to 42 g) butter

1 clove garlic, finely minced

1 scallion, finely minced

¼ cup (60 ml) chicken broth

1 cup (250 ml) dry white wine (like a Pinot Grigio)

1 tablespoon (15 ml) Rosanna's Tomato Sauce (PAGE 172) or pureed tomato

2 ounces (57 g) Italian prosciutto, cut into ½-inch (1.3 cm) cubes

½ cup (118 ml) heavy cream, at room temperature

8 ounces (227 g) dried or fresh spinach linguine, any Italian brand

8 ounces (227 g) dried or fresh plain linguine, any Italian brand

½ cup (75 g) shelled fresh peas or frozen baby peas

Sea salt

Parmigiano-Reggiano cheese, in one piece for grating

In a large sauté pan, combine the oil and butter and place over medium heat. When the butter has melted, add the garlic and scallion. Sauté for 3 minutes, watching carefully so the garlic doesn't burn. Add the broth and wine and bring to a simmer. Add the tomato sauce and peas. Cook for about 5 minutes, until the sauce has reduced slightly. Add the prosciutto and cook for 5 minutes longer. Remove from the heat and set aside.

Meanwhile, cook the pastas together in a large pot of boiling salted water until al dente (with a little give). Drain in a colander.

Put half of the sauce in the pasta pot, then return the pasta to the pot and top with remaining vegetable mixture and the cream. Toss to combine the pasta and vegetables, adding salt to taste if necessary. Grate cheese over the top and serve immediately.

Pork Loin Chops

In Italy, meat is served as an accompaniment to vegetables and starches, not the other way around. This recipe, using thin pork chops (ask your butcher to cut them extra thin to imitate the delicate European cut) is a perfect way to reduce the amount of meat consumed at dinner. The homemade bread crumbs that coat the pork chop became tasty and crunchy after being sautéed in olive oil. This is one of my daughters' favorite meals: It's simple and extremely flavorful, great with a spring vegetable like fresh peas or asparagus in the oven and red potatoes (SEE RECIPES, PAGES 32 AND 35). Pour an Italian sparkling Prosecco wine.

SERVES 4

1 egg, beaten in a shallow dish

1 cup (50 g) toasted bread crumbs, preferably from a hearty Italian bread (SEE NOTE)

Sea salt and freshly ground black pepper

4 boneless ¾-inch-thick (2 cm) pork loin chops

¼ cup (60 ml) extra-virgin olive oil

Put the egg and bread crumbs in separate shallow dishes. Season them with salt and pepper to taste.

Dip the pork chops in the egg and turn to coat both sides. Dredge in the bread crumbs, turning to coat both sides, and set the chops aside on a plate. Heat the oil in a large sauté pan over medium-high heat until the oil is hot but not smoking. Place the chops in the pan and cook until golden brown on both sides and the inside is no longer pink when tested with a knife, about 5 minutes on each side. Serve immediately.

NOTE: *To make fresh toasted bread crumbs: toast 4 large slices of day-old bread in the oven at 300°F (149°C) (Gas mark 2) until golden. Cut into large chunks and pulse in a food processor until finely chopped. (If you do not have a food processor you can chop the bread with a knife.)*

Wild Alaskan Sockeye Salmon

One of my favorite meals to make features wild salmon caught in the Pacific Northwest. This delicious and extremely nutritious treat is filled with vitamins and essentials oils that are so good for your body. As an added bonus, this fish is very easy and quick to cook. When you purchase the salmon, make sure it doesn't smell fishy (that means it's not fresh).

SERVES 4

1 ½ pounds (680 g) wild salmon fillet, with skin

1 clove garlic, crushed but left whole

¼ cup (60 ml) extra-virgin olive oil

1 tablespoon (15 ml) freshly squeezed lemon juice

Sea salt

Rub the fish all over with the garlic; discard the garlic. Drizzle the oil and lemon juice over the fish and season with salt to taste. Cover and refrigerate until ready to bake, ideally for about 2 hours.

Preheat the oven to 350°F (177°C) (Gas mark 4).

Place the salmon on a broiler pan, skin side down. Bake until flesh flakes easily when prodded with a knife, 8 to 9 minutes per inch of thickness for medium-rare (with a slightly translucent pink center). If you prefer well-done fish, cook for 10 minutes per inch of thickness. Serve immediately.

Pork Rib Roast with Fresh Herbs and Sea Salt

This pork roast is typical of those enjoyed in the Italian regions of Umbria and Lazio, and for Italians it means that spring has arrived. Start marinating the pork a day in advance. Have the butcher french the ribs on the roast (clean off the bones), leaving the roast in one piece. Plan on serving one rib per person, but order a couple of extra ribs for those who want seconds. Serve the roast with Asparagus in the Oven and California Brown Rice (SEE RECIPES, PAGES 32 AND 34).

SERVES 6

3 large sprigs fresh rosemary, stemmed

4 large sprigs fresh sage, stemmed

5 large cloves garlic

2 teaspoons (12 g) sea salt, plus more to taste

2 slices freshly cut Italian prosciutto, minced

½ cup (120 ml) extra-virgin olive oil

1 (7- or 8-rib) pork rib roast, frenched

On a board, chop the herbs and garlic together with the salt to form a coarse paste. Put the paste in a small bowl and stir in the prosciutto and ¼ cup (60 ml) of the oil.

Place the roast in a baking pan and with a sharp knife make deep slits directly into the meat on the top and bottom. With a teaspoon, stuff the herb mixture into the slits. Rub some of the herb mixture all over the outside of the roast as well. Drizzle the roast with the remaining ¼ cup (60 ml) oil. Liberally season with sea salt all over the roast, cover, and let marinate in the refrigerator overnight. Remove from the refrigerator 30 minutes before roasting.

Preheat the oven to 350°F (177°C) (Gas mark 4).

Roast the pork for 30 minutes per pound, or until the pork registers 170°F (76°C) on an instant-read meat thermometer, basting often with the juices from the pan.

Either bring the dramatic roast whole to the table for carving, or cut it between the rib bones into serving pieces (one rib per serving). Drizzle the meat with the pan juices and serve immediately.

Butterscotch Pie

This pie, with its lush, deep tones of butterscotch, has been a favorite of my family's since my mother began making it for us when we were little. The pie has its roots in the South, where many desserts feature brown sugar as the star ingredient. After all these years, I still find this pie lip-smacking delicious. We inevitably end up using our fingers to wipe the last bit of cream and homemade crust from the dessert plate.

MAKES 1 (9-INCH) (23 CM) PIE; SERVES 6 TO 8

½ recipe (1 ball) My Mom's Extra-Flaky Pie Crust Dough (PAGE 138)

4 large egg yolks

1½ cups (355 ml) whole milk

1 cup (236 ml) heavy cream

1 cup (172 g) brown sugar, firmly packed

¼ teaspoon (1.5 g) salt

3 tablespoons (42 g) salted butter

½ teaspoon (2.5 ml) vanilla extract

Sweetened vanilla whipped cream (SEE NOTE)

Preheat the oven to 350°F (177°C) (Gas mark 4). Roll the dough out into a circle ⅛ inch (3 mm) thick and fit it into a 9-inch (23 cm) pie pan. Trim and flute the edge. Line with parchment paper and fill with dried beans, rice, or metal pie weights. Bake for 20 minutes, until browned. Transfer to a wire rack to cool completely.

In a small bowl, beat the egg yolks until they are lemon-yellow. Set aside.

In a small pot, bring the milk and cream to the scalding point; you'll know the cream has reached the right temperature when a "skin" forms on top of the liquid.

Meanwhile, in the top of a double boiler over simmering water, combine the brown sugar, salt, and butter. Stir until the butter is melted and the mixture is completely blended. Gradually pour the hot milk mixture into the brown sugar mixture, stirring constantly.

Pour a little bit of the warm double-boiler mixture into the egg yolks. Mix well, then return the mixture to the double boiler. Cook over medium-high heat, stirring constantly with a whisk, until the custard thickens, 15 to 20 minutes; remember that it will firm up as it cools. Beat until smooth, then stir in the vanilla.

Pour into the pie shell and smooth the top. Cover with wax paper and refrigerate until cold. Spread the whipped cream in a thick layer over the custard. Serve, and wait for your guests' responses. This is a showstopper.

NOTE: *Make the whipped cream at the last minute. Using an electric mixer, beat 1 pint (472 ml) cold heavy cream, gradually adding ¼ cup (30 g) confectioners' sugar, beating constantly. Beat in 1 teaspoon (5 ml) vanilla extract as the cream thickens. Beat until the cream holds semi firm peaks.*

Coconut Cream Pie

This delectable cream pie is a wonderful mixture of lightly toasted coconut and dense homemade cream base with hints of velvety vanilla. I love the combination of the slightly salty crust, the creamy filling, and the crunch of the toasted coconut. This pie makes a lovely spring dessert and a culinary treat.

MAKES 1 (9-INCH) (23 CM) PIE; SERVES 6 TO 8

½ recipe (1 ball) My Mom's Extra-Flaky Pie Crust Dough (PAGE 138)

1½ cups (114 g) shredded sweetened coconut

5 large eggs, beaten

2½ cups (592 ml) whole milk

¾ cup (150 g) sugar

¼ cup (32 g) cornstarch

¼ teaspoon (1.5 g) fine sea salt

3 to 5 tablespoons (42 to 70 g) unsalted butter, cut into small cubes

1½ tablespoons (22 ml) vanilla

Preheat the oven to 350°F (177°C) (Gas mark 4). Roll the dough out to a circle ⅛ inch (3 mm) thick and fit it into a 9-inch (23 cm) pie pan. Trim and flute the edge. Line with parchment paper and fill with dried beans, rice, or metal pie weights. Bake for 20 minutes, until browned. Transfer to a wire rack to cool completely.

Lower the oven temperature to 300°F (149°C) (Gas mark 2).

Spread the coconut on a baking sheet. Toast until golden brown, 5 to 7 minutes. Let cool to room temperature.

In a medium bowl, using an electric mixer, beat the eggs until light yellow. Set aside.

In a small saucepan, bring the milk to the scalding point; you'll know the milk has reached the right temperature when a "skin" forms on top of the liquid.

In the top of a double boiler off the heat, whisk together the sugar, cornstarch, and salt, then whisk in the heated milk until thoroughly combined. Put the pan over simmering water in the bottom part of the double boiler, then gradually add the beaten eggs, stirring constantly with a wooden spoon. Remove from the heat and blend in the butter with an electric mixer. Stir in the vanilla.

Stir in 1¼ cups (127 g) of the toasted coconut, then spoon the mixture into the cooled pie shell and top with the remaining coconut. Cover with wax paper and refrigerate until cold. Serve.

Cindy's Bunny Cake

When we were little, every year around Easter, my mother made Bunny Cake to celebrate my sister's April birthday and the arrival of spring. I find that Dr. Oetker's organic vanilla cake mix works very well here, but if you prefer to make homemade cake use the layers from my Grandma's Caramel Cake (SEE RECIPE, PAGE 139). Be creative with your choice of colors—you can make a pastel bunny or opt for brighter colors, or go with all white. Decorate the serving plate with fresh flowers and spring greenery just before serving. This cake makes a great centerpiece and is a wonderful way to welcome spring.

SERVES 6 TO 8

¾ cup (1½ sticks) (170 g) unsalted butter

4 cups (452 g) confectioners' sugar

½ cup (118 ml) heavy cream

1 teaspoon (5 ml) vanilla extract

⅛ teaspoon (.7 ml) salt

3 tablespoons (45 ml) whole milk (if necessary)

1 (8-inch) (20 cm) round white cake layer, cooled to room temperature (SEE HEADNOTE)

2 cups (152 g) sweetened shredded coconut

Jelly beans or other candies, for eyes and nose

Paper ears made from charming spring wrapping paper

Large-leafed greenery such as lilac leaves, to surround the bunny

In a large bowl with an electric mixer, cream the butter until very light and fluffy. Add the confectioners' sugar and cream and beat until smooth. Beat in the vanilla and salt. If the frosting is too thick, beat in the milk, 1 tablespoon (15 ml) at a time.

Cut the cake layer in half to make 2 semicircles. Spread the top of one semicircle with frosting and place the second on top. Stand the semicircle upright on a serving platter so the rounded side is up. Cut a small triangle out of one side and put it where the tail of the bunny would be (SEE DIAGRAM).

Starting with the sides of the cake, spread the remaining frosting all over the bunny, being careful when you frost the cut areas of the cake so it doesn't crumble. Gently take handfuls of coconut and generously pat it all over the frosted bunny. Stick jelly beans onto the frosting to make eyes. Stick the ears in place. Surround the bunny with greenery and serve.

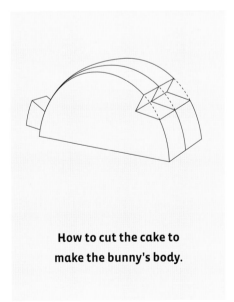

How to cut the cake to make the bunny's body.

Pat's Biscuits and Sugar Butter

This recipe has its origins in the pioneer era and has been handed down through four generations in my family. My mother's classic biscuit is very much like the version that is eaten widely throughout the South. I believe that the sugar butter may come from Virginia, where my great-grandparents settled after emigrating from Wales. Like many truly great recipes, this is one that has survived many generations and carries with it the love with which the food is made.

The saltiness of the biscuit with the praline flavor of the sugar-butter syrup is a taste treat not to be missed. Serve with scrambled eggs and fresh bacon. Set your table with special "Sunday breakfast" dishes that you use every Sunday. To round out the meal, brew a pot of good-quality black tea or fresh coffee.

For a shorter, richer biscuit, use 6 tablespoons (80 g) butter in the dough. For a lighter, airier biscuit, use just 4 tablespoons (60 g).

MAKES 12 BISCUITS

1¾ cups (233 g) all-purpose flour

2½ teaspoons (15 g) baking powder

1 teaspoon (6 g) fine sea salt

4 to 6 tablespoons (56 to 84 g) salted butter, at room temperature, plus 3 tablespoons (42 g) melted butter

⅔ to 1 cup (188 to 250 ml) whole milk

Accompaniments: butter, jam, marmalade, and Sugar Butter (SEE RIGHT)

Preheat the oven to 450°F (232°C) (Gas mark 8). Grease a baking sheet.

Put the flour, baking powder, and salt in a food processor and pulse to combine. Add the room-temperature butter and pulse until the mixture is the consistency of cornmeal.

Add ⅔ cup (188 ml) milk and pulse just until combined; add more milk a little at a time, if necessary, to make a soft dough. When the dough forms one large ball, remove from the processor. Lightly knead the dough on a floured board for 30 seconds, roughly 10 folds. The dough should be moist and light; heavy dough will make tough biscuits—again, avoid overworking the dough. Gently form the dough into a ball and roll it out ½ inch (1.3 cm) thick on a floured board using a floured rolling pin. Cut the biscuits with a round biscuit cutter or other fun-shaped cutters, or with a mid-sized drinking glass. Put all the biscuits on the prepared baking sheet. Give the dough scraps to young children to make miniature biscuits using a 1 ½-inch (4 cm) cookie cutter or a shot glass.

Brush the tops of the biscuits with the melted butter. Bake for 12 to 15 minutes, until lightly browned. Remove from the oven, but keep the biscuits on the baking sheet until ready to serve. Serve on a tiered compote with butter, jam, marmalade, and Sugar Butter. Cut the biscuits in half and ladle the sugar butter over the buttered biscuit.

Sugar Butter

MAKES ENOUGH FOR 12 BISCUITS

1 cup (2 sticks) (226 g) salted butter

1 cup (172 g) brown sugar

½ cup (118 ml) heavy cream, or more if necessary

In a small saucepan over medium heat, melt the butter, then stir in the brown sugar and cook until the mixture bubbles. Add the cream, and turn down the heat to keep the cream just below a simmer. Cook for about 10 minutes on low heat, until the sugar is dissolved and the flavors are balanced. The syrup will be creamy in texture. If you need more, just add a bit more cream. Transfer the sugar butter to a gravy boat–type server. Use a small gravy ladle to serve the syrup.

Sleepover Chocolate Chip Pancakes

These pancakes are the perfect breakfast for a pre teen sleepover party. They are homemade and deliciously decadent served with pure Vermont maple syrup. After a long night of chatting and girl talk, this breakfast is the perfect food to accompany the last bit of silliness and joking before everyone heads home. To offset the rich, high-carbohydrate breakfast, I serve tall glasses of ice-cold organic 2 percent milk (then leave the girls to enjoy the meal on their own). Use several skillets so guests are not left waiting for their breakfasts.

MAKES 8 (6-INCH) (15 CM) PANCAKES

1 cup (142 g) all-purpose flour

¼ cup (49 g) sugar

1 teaspoon (6 g) fine sea salt

1 teaspoon (6 g) baking powder

1 cup (250 ml) whole milk

2 large eggs

1 teaspoon (5 ml) vanilla extract

3 tablespoons (42 g) butter, melted

Canola oil

1 (10-ounce) (284 g) bag semisweet chocolate chips (you want to add about 7 or 8 chips per pancake)

Real Vermont maple syrup, for serving

Mix the flour, sugar, salt, and baking powder together in a large mixing bowl and set aside. In another bowl, whisk together the milk, eggs, vanilla, and butter. Gently pour the wet ingredients into the dry and fold to just combine.

Brush a large, heavy skillet (or several skillets) with oil, then place over medium-high heat. Using a ¼-cup (12 ml) measuring cup, scoop the batter into the skillet to form 6-inch (15 cm) pancakes. Cook until small bubbles appear on the top of the pancake, then sprinkle with chocolate chips. Flip the pancake to cook the other side until lightly browned or golden, about 4 minutes per side, or until the top is bubbling and the bottom has solidified. Serve hot, with syrup.

As the cupcakes are cooling make the frosting. In a large bowl, using an electric mixer, cream the butter until very light. Add the confectioners' sugar and 3 tablespoons (45 ml) of the milk and beat until smooth. Add the vanilla, salt, and food coloring, adding more or less coloring depending on how pink you want the frosting. If the frosting is too thick, thin it with a little more milk. Beat until smooth. Frost the cooled cupcakes and serve on tiered cake pedestals. Garnish with a pastel candle in each cupcake.

Homemade Popcorn in a Pan

My grandmother made popcorn like this for me when I was a child. I love its homemade flavor and authentic popcorn taste. It has been a favorite of my family's for years.

MAKES 1 LARGE SOUP KETTLE FULL OF POPCORN

¼ cup (½ stick) (57 g) butter

¼ cup (60 ml) canola oil

Sea salt

½ cup (106 g) popcorn

Melt half of the butter in a small saucepan and set aside.

In a large, heavy-bottomed pot, heat the oil and the remaining butter over high heat until the butter is melted. Add salt to taste, then add the popcorn. Cover and cook over medium-high heat. When the corn starts popping, shake the pan vigorously to prevent the popcorn from burning. When the popping sounds slow down, lower the heat to medium and continue to cook and shake the pan vigorously until the popping stops. Pour half of the popcorn into a large bowl, and then drizzle with some of the melted butter and season with more salt if necessary. Repeat with the remaining popcorn and butter. Serve with lots of napkins, and be careful—once you start eating this delicious popcorn, you won't be able to stop.

Cupcakes

Dr. Oetker–brand organic cake mixes are available in gourmet or health food stores, some supermarkets, and online. With a good mix, homemade cupcakes are easy to pull off, even for a busy mom.

MAKES 24 CUPCAKES

Cupcakes made from 1 box each Dr. Oetker Organics vanilla and chocolate cake mixes, cooled completely

6 tablespoons (¾ stick) (84 g) butter

2 cups (226 g) confectioners' sugar

About ¼ cup (60 ml) whole milk

1 teaspoon (5 ml) vanilla extract

⅛ teaspoon (.7 g) salt

1 or 2 drops red food coloring

summer

Let simplicity and

gracious living
be your guide.

In our fast-paced world, we long for connections with others on the most basic level. Summertime is the perfect time to reestablish contact with our friends and with nature. It's a magical time that allows us to release our inhibitions, exhibited by the clothes we wear, the food we eat, and the slowed pace of our lives. Borrow from the past to resurrect good-neighbor relationships and establish a rapport with those who are a part of your daily life.

When I was a child, it was customary to stop by a neighbor's home unannounced for a cup of coffee. People enjoyed long chats over a fence between houses. Sometimes, that chat would lead to an invitation to come over for iced tea, lemonade, or, in the late afternoon, a mug of beer. Today, the neighborhoods feel empty during the summer. Very few yards bear the mark of outdoor living. No children laughing and playing, no people gardening, not even the friendly hum of an electric lawn mower. There is only silence. Empty neighborhoods in summertime make for a strange and lonely landscape.

People are naturally drawn to spending time with other people. It lessens the loneliness of the human condition.

In many places in the world, this scenario would not exist. Over the past ten years I've spent part of each summer in Italy. During my time there, I've observed that, unlike in the United States, people in Italy don't need much encouragement to come together. People set up folding chairs outside apartment buildings, and from this vantage point engage in long conversations as they enjoy the goings-on of the neighborhood. This ritual allows Italians to connect with each other on a daily basis.

People are naturally drawn to spending time with other people. It lessens the loneliness of the human condition. It makes us feel vital and engaged in the world. The Italians have known this for ages, and their way of life is exemplified by the town square, *la piazza*, which functions as a communal living room during the evening. The piazza is an open, lively space perpetually teeming with people. No generation is left out; every age is present and included in the lively celebration of life. You'll see children playing soccer, young people strolling along in couples or groups, and older people sitting in the cafés enjoying the scene. The permanent fixture of an Italian piazza is the group of elderly men and women chatting animatedly about politics, family life, or the latest juicy gossip.

Everyone takes part in the daily ritual of socializing, even the shopkeepers, who close their stores promptly at 7:30. Other than a small glass of wine or apéritif before dinner, there's no shopping—no frantic consumption of goods. The custom of closing shops early focuses everyone's attention on interacting with each other. This interaction encourages people to join in community life in a meaningful way because, once the stores close, the best entertainment available is to enjoy the pleasure of eating and drinking together, watching and listening as life goes by. During the summer months, it's much easier for us to emulate the Italians. We can avoid covered shopping malls and commercial areas that make shopping the main event. Our world is filled with many places that enrich us intellectually and physically and cost little or nothing—parks, museums, botanical gardens, or national monuments are just a few places that encourage interaction with others. Going outside your home and striking up a conversation with a neighbor is another way to interact. Turning on the sprinkler and letting the children run through it encourages spontaneous play. The sound of children's laughter is a balm to the weary heart and brings joy to all who hear it. Connecting, reaching out, and experiencing life will help you establish a deep appreciation for the world around you, and that in turn will do wonders for your sense of well-being and contentment.

Make the Most of All Five Senses

In the Italian language, one of the most important words used on a daily basis is *sentire*, "to feel."
Sentire does not imply only "feeling" in the literal sense. Rather, this word encompasses all five of
the senses. It's not uncommon when eating with an Italian to hear *"Vuoi sentire questo?"*—"Do you
want to taste [feel or experience] this?" This expression revels in the fact that we experience the
world as a series of sensations. When we eat, we don't simply taste flavor with our taste buds.
We use all of our senses to appreciate food. We smell its aroma, see its form, feel its texture, hear
its crunch. If we focus on all of our senses, life takes on more richness. The small moments we
experience every day become more important, and life becomes a feast to enjoy with gusto. It is
in recognizing the small moments of pleasure that true happiness is found.

      During the summer months, make an extra effort to stay in touch with all of your senses.
Engaging with our senses is an important part of living a full and satisfying life. When I visit Italy in
the summer, I notice how it's much easier for me to stay aware of my senses, and that knowledge
infuses my soul with a meaningful sense of happiness.

Use Your Sense of Sight

The Italians love to watch life go by. They make a ritual out of looking. Cities are planned around the piazza to allow people to gather, connect, and, most importantly, to see and be seen. Numerous sidewalk cafés provide the perfect place for the Italians to practice one of their favorite pastimes: surveying the banquet of life. By watching, the Italians become active participants in living. By looking at people and allowing ourselves to be looked at, we reaffirm each other's existence. Being looked at makes us feel human; it makes us feel like we matter.

Try to incorporate the art of taking notice into your daily routine. Enjoy the visual feast of life.

The taste and smell of Italian produce is intoxicating, ensuring dining experiences that frequently border on transcendent.

Use Your Senses of Taste and Smell

Italy is one of the places in the world where good, fresh food has always played a central part in living a quality life. The taste and smell of Italian produce is intoxicating, ensuring dining experiences that frequently border on transcendent.

It's rare to find a fruit or a vegetable in a market when the variety is out of season. Tomatoes, for example, are at their best in Italy in the late spring and early summer. Most of the tomatoes in Italian markets come from Sicily, where the hot and sunny climate produces fruits bursting with flavor. When tomatoes are at their peak, Italians make great batches of *passato al pomodoro* (fresh bottled tomato sauce) to stockpile in their larders during the winter months when tomatoes and other vegetables are no longer in season.

You might think about getting the best tomatoes you can so you too can preserve the bounty of the seasonal produce and create a well-stocked pantry (SEE THE "IN MY KITCHEN" LIST, PAGE 68).

Canning in huge quantities—setting up a gas burner out in the yard for cooking enormous pots of tomato sauce, as many Italians in this country do at the height of the season, for example—might seem like a daunting task. Start with smaller batches—even six or eight pints of sauce will go a long way toward making at least a few of your meals feel fresh and summery in the wintertime. In addition, there are alternative, even less time-consuming ways to preserve food. I, for example, don't even can my tomato sauce (SEE RECIPE, PAGE 172). Instead, I make large batches, divide them among smaller containers the right size for individual meals, and put them in the freezer. That way, I ensure that my favorite pasta dishes will always have the taste of fresh-picked summer tomatoes.

Use Your Sense of Touch

It's an old joke, but it has a large measure of truth: Without their hands, Italians would be incapable of expressing themselves. Gesturing, raving, teasing, and, above all, embracing—Italians love to express themselves by touch. When you meet a friend in Italy, the first thing you do after saying hello is to embrace and offer two kisses, one on each cheek. This ritual is an expression that shows you care and share a connection.

Italian families demonstrate their love of touch when they communicate with their children. Mothers stroke their children's faces with deep affection and care. And who could forget the fact that Italy is notorious for lovers who kiss passionately in public without timidity or shame?

The sense of touch is evident everywhere in Italy, creating an atmosphere of warmth and welcome. We could all take a lesson from the Italians and loosen our own inhibitions.

When we meet a friend, we should let our affection shine through with a warm touch. Most importantly, when we are with our children, we should demonstrate our love with a warm embrace or a sweet kiss. Every child responds positively to touch, many times more so than if we express our feelings only with words. We should all strive for daily intimacies, and using our sense of touch to its fullest is one of the best ways to do that.

Six Ways to Integrate Touch into Daily Life

1. A Euro-style kiss, on one cheek or both, is a lovely and elegant way to greet a friend.

2. A handshake or a touch on the arm communicates trust and commitment.

3. A warm bear hug for family members demonstrates love of kin.

4. An arm around the shoulders or holding a hand shows commitment to a friendship during trying times.

5. A high-five for co-workers can be a wonderful sign of triumph and success at work.

6. Goodnight kisses and embraces are always a lovely way to send a child off to sleep and offer an expression of security before they drift into dreams.

Use Your Sense of Hearing

Are you listening to the rhythm of life? The music of the Italian street is magical. We hear the buzz of a Vespa, exuberant exclamations of happiness, and the constant whir of the espresso machine in the café downstairs. Conversations in the street sound like beautiful recitatives lifted straight out of scenes from the Italian operas. And, at any time of day, we hear the tolling of church bells, a sound that never fails to touch my soul.

What can we do in our lives to drink in this symphony of sound? Too often, we close off our audio world by listening to iPods or by talking on our cell phones. But by staying attentive to the sounds in our environment, we become part of the world on another level. To engage as active participants in life, we need to unplug. Open our windows and listen: The concert of life awaits.

Six Ways to Engage in the Beauty of Everyday Sound

1. Go to a park and just sit. Listen to the children laughing and playing, the dogs barking, the birds singing, and the leaves rustling. This is pure beauty.

2. Sit at an outdoor café and tune in to the buzz of the multiple conversations around you.

3. Go to an outdoor concert.

4. Stop and listen to a good musical performance by a street performer.

5. In the mornings, take time to listen to the birds chirping to each other.

6. Go for a walk in the woods and listen to the quiet mix of nature's movements and the green world growing.

Discover Beauty in Your Space

Italians live surrounded by breathtakingly beautiful art and thousands of years of history. These treasures and their heritage make the Italians deeply appreciative of the past and reverent of items crafted by hand. The phrase "throw-away culture" does not exist there. In Italy, old things are not thrown away but repaired and passed down from one generation to the next. The sense of what has come before is omnipresent.

One of my favorite pastimes in Italy is to visit the local open-air antiques and flea markets. Almost every weekend, one can find a market showcasing old treasures. A strong connection to the past is something we should practice in our own lives, in which oftentimes *new* means "better," and *old* means "passé." Treasuring one's history makes it possible to take the best from the past and reinvent it for the future. The appreciation of the old ensures a future that has the depth of soul necessary to thrive and produce wondrous new things.

What do you have in your closet and your family's closets that evokes your family's traditions? Do you have dishes from your family's past that were used yearly for a certain holiday meal? Is there a pair of candlesticks used for special family dinners? Does your grandmother or great-grandmother have any old damask table linens? No one makes damask these days, but one of the lovely characteristics of this fabric is a beautiful texture that comes only with age. Damask tablecloths are wonderful items with which to resurrect the ritual of sitting down to family dinners with linens. Are there any items like teapots, teacups and saucers, salad plates, old silver sugar bowls, or stemware that are sitting in your family's cupboard waiting to be incorporated into your mealtime rituals and traditions?

Shop Your Grandma's or Mother's Attic

Here is a list of great items to keep an eye out for that will help you restore family traditions in your own home.

1. Sets of old china (any period).

2. Sets of old ceramic ware (chunky everyday pottery in a solid color with a period design).

3. Silver candlesticks (plate or sterling).

4. Vintage floral porcelain cups and saucers.

5. Tablecloths, napkins, or runners made of lace, damask, linen, or printed cotton.

6. Crystal stemware (hand cut or plain).

7. Silverware (stainless steel, silver plate, or sterling silver flatware).

8. Sterling silver or silver plate sugar holders to use as small vases.

9. Dessert dishes or bowls made of porcelain or bone china for layering with solid china.

10. Vases or pitchers made of cut crystal, ceramic, or porcelain make wonderful centerpieces filled with flowers.

11. Oversized trays, in silver plate, painted papier-mâché, or tin, are dramatic for serving and useful for anchoring a centerpiece.

12. Any item that has a memory attached to it and is part of your own personal history—a figurine, an objet d'art, or an architectural implement.

13. Old Christmas ornaments and decorations passed down from family or friends.

14. Thanksgiving, Halloween, Easter, Passover, or other multicultural or religious artifacts that have been used in traditions over the years.

15. Antiques-shop and flea-market finds that speak to your heart and soul.

Stock Up: Ensure a Delicious Eating Experience Year Round

The ritual of gathering and stocking a pantry with quality food is one that dates back to the beginning of civilization. Borrowing the Italian practice of outfitting a bountiful pantry encourages us to remember our agricultural roots. In Italy, a great deal of effort goes into the gathering of the best and freshest ingredients from local farmers' markets, where you can find not just produce but high-quality olive oil. Find out where and when your local farmers' market is held and make a point of visiting it regularly. Increasingly there are local vineyards, just as there are in Italy, where you can find artisan food products and fresh produce in addition to wine. To reproduce some of the feeling of getting my food from a fresh Italian market, I rely on a local wholesale distributor that imports great Italian olive oil, pastas, vinegars, and cheeses.

Many Italian families have small, cool rooms filled with foodstuffs of excellent quality for the winter. With just a bit more effort, we can create a great daily eating experience by having good food at our fingertips as well. A pantry serves a number of important functions and also makes it easier to accommodate drop-in guests (SEE "BE READY FOR SPONTANEOUS GET-TOGETHERS," PAGE 70) and reduces the need to buy food on the run. Quality food satisfies one of our most basic needs: experiencing simple pleasures that nourish the body.

When I was a child, my mother preserved the bounty of late summer and fall by canning and freezing. She was a farm girl from Kansas and was keenly aware of traditional ways to provide the best and freshest food for her family. I remember many summertime trips to orchards in the country, where we picked buckets and buckets of ripe peaches for canning.

My mother also took advantage of the profusion of berry fields just outside our hometown of Portland, Oregon, where one could find boysenberries, raspberries, Marionberries, and blackberries. In fringed straw hats, Keds sneakers, and cut-off jeans, my two sisters and I headed east with our mother in an old Chevy sedan. My sister Vicky was the champion berry picker among us. At the end of the day, she always had the most flats of the delicious berries to show for her labors. My sister Cindy, like me, was more laid back, and more berries found their way to her mouth instead of into her basket. Still, at the end of the day we all returned home with hands stained inky black. The large flats of berries were gingerly put in our car for safe transport back home, where they were made into jams and jellies and frozen in batches just right for a midwinter treat of berry pie.

In My Kitchen

Stocking up on quality foods makes hosting a spontaneous dinner party easy. Here's a list of some essential ingredients that I always have on hand.

PANTRY BASICS

Extra-virgin olive oil

Canola oil

Aged balsamic vinegar from Italy

Red wine vinegar from Italy or France

4 (28-ounce/794 g) cans whole peeled San Marzano tomatoes* (SEE PAGES 172, 173)

4 (14-ounce/414 ml) cans Swanson's organic chicken broth

1 box Star-brand chicken bouillon cubes (YOU CAN FIND THESE AT ITALIAN GOURMET FOOD STORES)

PANTRY STARCHES

1 pound (454 g) penne rigate pasta, preferaby De Cecco brand

1 pound (454 g) linguine fini pasta, preferably De Cecco or Barilla brand

1 pound (454 g) orzo pasta

1 pound (454 g) stellette pasta, preferably De Cecco brand (SMALL STAR-SHAPED PASTA THAT'S DELICIOUS COOKED IN A SIMPLE BROTH)

1 pound (454 g) campanelle pasta, preferably Barilla brand (CURLY PASTA SHAPE THAT HOLDS SAUCE VERY WELL, CRADLING IT AND ENSURING THAT EACH PIECE IS WELL COATED, A WONDERFUL WAY TO SHOWCASE A GREAT SAUCE; SEE RECIPE, PAGE 89)

1 pound (454 g) Tsuru Mai California brown rice (DELICIOUS COOKED IN ORGANIC CHICKEN BROTH, WITH A LOVELY NUTTY FLAVOR AND TEXTURE THAT MARRIES NICELY WITH ALL KINDS OF MEATS; SEE RECIPE, PAGE 34)

1 pound (454 g) lentils

1 pound (454 g) 17-bean-and-barley mix (A GREAT ALTERNATIVE TO MEAT; CAN BE MADE INTO A DELICIOUS SOUP VERY EASILY)

STORAGE VEGETABLES

3 heads garlic

4 yellow onions

1 pound (454 g) small red potatoes

1 pound (454 g) baking potatoes

San Marzano tomatoes taste wonderful and are not hard to find. You can find them at Williams-Sonoma, Whole Foods, and other natural-food stores.

REFRIGERATOR CONDIMENTS

French Dijon mustard

Jar of small capers

Jar of mayonnaise made with olive oil and real eggs

Fresh herbs (I GROW MOST OF THESE IN MY GARDEN OUTSIDE)

   Rosemary

   Oregano

   Basil

   Laurel (bay) leaves

   Sage

   Marjoram

   Parsley

   Thyme

FRESH VEGETABLES

1 bunch celery

1 bunch carrots

2 heads romaine lettuce

2 red bell peppers

2 green bell peppers

Asparagus (IN SPRING)

Tomatoes (IN SUMMER)

Brussels sprouts (IN FALL)

Acorn squash (IN FALL)

Kale (IN WINTER)

DAIRY

1 gallon 2% milk

1 pint (472 ml) whipping cream (FOR SAUCES AND FROSTING)

1 pound (454 g) local cheddar cheese

1 pound (454 g) Parmigiano-Reggiano cheese

1 pound (454 g) fresh mozzarella balls

1 pound (454 g) quality butter

FREEZER

1 free-range whole chicken

16 loin lamb chops cut from rack of lamb, about 2 inches (5 cm) long (SEE RECIPE, PAGE 94)

8 boneless pork chops, ½ inch (1.3 cm) thick (SEE RECIPE, PAGE 39)

8 links mild Italian sausage (TURKEY, CHICKEN, OR PORK, MADE FRESH BY YOUR BUTCHER)

SPICE CUPBOARD

Peperoncini (TINY ITALIAN RED PEPPERS THAT ADD A KICK TO PASTA SAUCES AND MEATS)

French sea salt (COARSE, IN A GRINDER)

Black peppercorns (BEST QUALITY, IN A GRINDER)

*When we spend our vacation in Italy,
unplanned dinner parties play an
important part in the Italian experience.*

Be Ready for Spontaneous Get-Togethers

Italians love to get together to eat, but Italian dinner parties are rarely formal affairs. After a genial conversation or a chance meeting with friends, both parties agree on a date a few days hence, and a dinner party is born. I love this facet of Italian culture. The invitation to an easygoing and relatively unexpected dinner party creates an atmosphere of exuberant anticipation, giving the evening a youthful, carefree freshness and providing an opportunity to enliven the spirit. When we spend our vacations in Italy, unplanned dinner parties play an important part in the Italian experience.

Our friend Vito recently remodeled his childhood home, adding an authentic outdoor wood-burning pizza oven. One evening at a spur-of-the-moment dinner at our home, he and his friend Daniela invited us over for a pizza party to inaugurate Vito's new oven. When we arrived at Vito's, we were surprised and pleased to see his entire family in attendance—his father and mother, sisters, brothers-in-law, nieces, nephews, and Daniela's sons adding to the festivity of the moment.

Vito and Daniela had marinated and displayed farm-fresh local produce in individual serving dishes, showcasing the bounty of summertime in Italy. Luscious grilled zucchini and eggplant drizzled with olive oil waited for Vito and Daniela to artfully drape them atop the pizzas, and the sight of pale baby onions, peppery green arugula, and sweet golden potato cubes made our mouths water.

Grated Parmigiano-Reggiano lay in great, fluffy mounds ready to be scooped up. They had also set out slices of mozzarella di bufala, sitting in pools of milky white liquid, for topping the pizzas. Unique artisanal cheeses such as pecorino fresco and pecorino stagionato (aged pecorino), procured from local cheesemakers, gave off a nutty aroma.

We thought we had taken in everything until we saw the cured-meat selection. Copious amounts of proscuitto di Norcia covered a large oval tray. Razor-thin slices of salumi, pancetta, and capocollo lay fanned out on a wooden board. Great, lusty chunks of grilled Umbrian sausage filled a hand-painted ceramic bowl.

As an antipasto prior to the pizzas, Vito and Daniela served a palate teaser: focaccia with pecorino and a fruity, dry white wine from the region of Marche. Salty and brushed with olive oil, the pizza dough was transformed into a completely different and flavor-laden treat. Our cooks delivered huge trays to our table accompanied by black wine-cured olives and small, briny green olives that made a fine contrast with the wine and bread. The focaccia was perfection: soft as a pillow, salty, with the golden kiss of olive oil. We devoured the whole platter in seconds.

Soon afterward, pizza after pizza topped with exquisite combinations of ingredients came to the table in an unending stream: grilled zucchini; proscuitto and artichoke; four cheeses; arugula and succulent Umbrian sausage. "Oohhs" and "ahhs" in English and Italian floated above the lively conversation, as we tasted one pizza after another. Just when we thought we couldn't eat another bite, Vito and Daniela came to our table, their immaculate white clothes smudged all over with soot from the labor of love. They announced that there was one more pizza coming. We all protested that we'd already had the taste experience of a lifetime. No, they insisted, this was one pizza we'd never forget. And they were right. What we were about to eat would send shivers from the tops of our heads to the tips of our toes: Nutella pizza.

Nutella is to the Italian what peanut butter is to the American, but a million times better. Nutella is a jarred spread made of roasted hazelnuts, cocoa, sugar, butter, and milk. Ask any Italian about Nutella. In response, you'll get the universal indication of ecstasy: eyes rolled back, and a facial expression of sheer bliss.

Now you can imagine our experience of Nutella pizza. This pizza was simply prepared: Daniela's amazing dough was sprinkled with sugar, then placed in the wood-burning oven until the sugar caramelized. Once the sugar melted, Daniela spread thick, creamy gobs of Nutella on the pizza. The hazelnut spread melted from the heat of the warm crust, creating a gooey, runny confection against the crisp, light dough. We thought we had died and gone to heaven. The texture! The taste! It was a moment beyond words.

We left that evening amazed that this life-changing dinner party had been planned only a day before. We had experienced so much: friendship, the coming together of two cultures, and a meal that touched the depths of our souls. It was an evening that, for me, forever changed the meaning of the phrase "dinner party."

Have Your Own Spontaneous Pizza Party

- Pick up the telephone and call your friends and invite them to a pizza party that night.

- Many pizza restaurants sell their dough raw; if you don't have time to make your own dough, ask around at your favorite pizzeria.

- Use a pizza stone to replicate the effect of pizza cooked in an authentic pizza oven. Preheat it as the oven comes up to a temperature of 500 – 550°F (260 – 288°C) (Gas mark 9), and let it heat for at least 30 minutes before you slide the first pizza onto it. Bake your pizza for 6 – 7 minutes, or until the crust is browned and bubbly.

- Use my tomato sauce recipe (PAGE 172) as a base sauce for the pizza.

- Use fresh mozzarella—the kind that comes in balls packed in water—as your first layer.

- Grate real Parmigiano-Reggiano in a food processor or with a Microplane grater to sprinkle on top.

- Use freshly sliced prosciutto, salami, or capocollo meats. Make sure your cold cuts are fresh and moist. Arrange the meats on top of the pizza after it has come out of the oven to avoid overcooking.

- Lightly sauté slices of zucchini, eggplant, and artichoke hearts in extra-virgin olive oil. Drain on paper towels and set aside to use as pizza toppings.

- Set out a jar of Nutella and have a small bowl of sugar ready to make an amazing dessert pizza.

- There are many great toppings you can use on your pizzas. See page 88 for more ideas.

- Have fun!

Fall in Love with a Place

When I was twenty years old, I studied abroad in Perugia, Italy. It was my junior year in college, and I was discovering, for the first time, the treasures of Italian life.

One day, I walked through the doors of a quiet pastry shop called Sandri. I ordered a cappuccino, took one sip, and fell in *love*. As I looked around, I discovered a world of mouthwatering pastries, aromatic coffees, and Italian delicacies that I'd never tasted before. I understood, after one bite, why people love Italian food. I was hooked, and there was nothing to be done—I was bound to this place for life. My love affair with Sandri has spanned three decades. My connection with this place and its food is a physical bond I feel in my core. Every year when I return, it feels like coming home.

One of my favorite summertime treats from Sandri is *granita di caffe con panna*. Granita is an Italian summer specialty made of flavored shaved ice. You can find granitas all over Italy, but a granita from Sandri is probably the only one that will, without fail, induce an out-of-body experience. The granita itself is made of delicate shards of ice carefully flavored with Sandri espresso and kissed with a touch of homemade sugar syrup. The drink is topped off with luscious whipped cream, thick and barely sweetened. The secret is in Sandri's hand-roasted coffee—a rich, dark espresso laced with notes of caramel that, like a fine wine, is worthy of being savored slowly. In the granita, the interplay of textures on the tongue transforms the experience of coffee drinking into a rare moment of transcendence. The richness of the high-quality cream and the slight bitterness of the coffee marry as the ice slivers dissolve slowly in your mouth. It excites the palate and cools the body on a hot summer afternoon, and as the caffeine clears away weariness and gives renewed energy to a tired body. One time, I ate three Sandri granitas in one day, returning sheepishly three separate times to order "just one more." Each time I came back, I ducked my head a little in shame. The waiter just looked at me and smiled. I simply love this treat.

After all these years of finding nourishment at Sandri, the waiters have befriended me and my family. One waiter from my college days, now officially in retirement, nevertheless makes several weekly trips to *il laboratorio* (the kitchen). He still remembers me as the twenty-year-old who could afford only the occasional *cappuccino al banco* (a cappuccino taken standing at the bar)—in Italy, as soon as you sit down at a table, the prices on the menu double. As a poor student, I was always standing at the counter sipping a cappuccino as a reward after long hours of studying. I cherish the history I share with this place.

Sandri is famous for so many pastries, it would be impossible to do all of their award-winning creations justice. But there's one other Sandri dish that is so special to me that I've incorporated it into my own family traditions. *Torta rustica*, Italian egg, ham, and cheese tart (SEE RECIPE, PAGE 166). After years of experimentation, I've come close to replicating this savory treat. A delicious puff pastry crust is filled with ricotta cheese, grated Parmigiano-Reggiano Proscuitto, and eggs, then baked in the oven until golden brown. The result is a multitextured delicacy of buttery, flaky crust, salty Italian ham, and creamy ricotta filling complemented by sharp, nutty grains of Parmesan. The contrast of the crisp pastry against the cheesy, salty filling is a voluptuous complete sensory experience. I've incorporated this dish into my holiday menu, and it has since become a family favorite. It makes me happy to have contributed a recipe to our family history, and it pleases me that I'm blending two cultures in the process.

The love of a place can broaden your world. It can take you somewhere you normally would not go. Sandri is a place I love. It has broadened my vision of what pleasure can mean. It has taught me how great food can nourish both the body and the spirit. It is a place I will cherish forever.

Find a place that you love and return again and again. It will serve as a storehouse of happy memories and good feelings. Each time you return, you will find that inspiration and renewal await you.

Make a Place Your Own

*All of us want a "third place," like a great café, restaurant, or bar,
where we can go on a regular basis and be recognized and appreciated—and, of course, enjoy
fabulous food and drink. Here are some tips for finding your own special spot.*

~ Find a place relatively close to home. Easy access is the key to frequent visits and quick bonding with the waiters and owners.

~ Pick a place that makes something that you simply love to eat, something that you could not replicate at home. I love Sandri because many of its famous delicacies are made from classic recipes unique to this pastry shop. For example, its *granita di caffe* is a singular dessert the likes of which I've never encountered anywhere else. One of the reasons I go back often is because I look forward to eating this amazing treat. When you pick a place, choose somewhere that offers an experience that is truly special and unique.

~ Select a place that makes you feel instantly at home. Seek out a space with an ambiance that invites you in and soothes your psyche, a place that makes you feel calm, safe, and welcome. You'll know when you've found the right place because it will feel like sinking into a big overstuffed club chair with a relieved "Ahhhh."

~ Finally, and most importantly, pick a place that makes you feel special and appreciated as soon as you walk through the door. Make sure the waiters and chefs take notice of you, and show them your appreciation with a warm greeting, a touch on the arm, or a handshake. Reaching out yourself does wonders for inspiring a welcome filled with warmth and hospitality.

Blend Cultures to Create Your Own

From the end of June to the middle of July, we live in an old farmhouse nestled in the hills of Umbria, Italy. Our sojourn in the countryside is an unusual one. During this time, we live a life half American, half Italian, and create our world using of the best of both cultures. Art, historical architecture, and the breathtaking natural beauty of the land surround us. Assisi, Perugia, Spoleto, and Orvieto, cultural centers that date back to antiquity, are all short drives away. I'm always struck by Umbria's profound beauty, which only deepens with the passage of time. I revere this region's rich culture and the people who live there, the guardians of its past.

Over the years, the Fourth of July has become a special part of our family's vacation. For us, celebrating Independence Day is not just an excuse to wave the American flag. Instead, we celebrate this quintessential American holiday by paying special attention to our connection with Italy. To honor this cross-cultural bond, I've created a unique Fourth of July celebration that blends the customs and traditions of America and Italy.

For the American element, I send over loads of Rosanna dishes from my company that I later give away as gifts to our guests. The table decorations provide an outlet for my creativity and an opportunity to express my pride in my American roots. I hand-carry vintage U.S. flags in my luggage, some so old that they have only forty-eight stars. I hang these flags on the terrace next to a large Italian flag as a testament to our respect for and connection to our host country.

I plan the dinner menu with great care to create a bicultural eating experience, and every year our friend Vito brings a gigantic cake festooned with the American flag. Though emblazoned in red, white, and blue, the cake itself is made in the Italian style: flaky puff pastry layered with delicious homemade pastry cream.

On past Fourth of July celebrations, I've used pale blue Rosanna dinner plates and topped them with red polka-dot eight-inch appetizer plates. I insert a small American flag in each napkin tied with ribbon at each place setting. I also give each guest an American flag baseball cap or T-shirt at the end of the evening. For a tablecloth, I typically use unhemmed Americana yardage I've found. I gather lavender from the countryside and bright yellow sunflowers to place in Rosanna recycled blue Mexican glass hurricanes as vases. I place a variety of small vintage flags around the house to create the festive spirit of the holiday. The idea is to create an American feeling that's enhanced by the beauty of the Italian countryside.

During the meal itself, I highlight the best of both countries by placing classic American and Umbrian dishes side by side. According to Italian custom, I serve the meal in multiple courses. *Il primo piatto*, the first course, is a pasta dish, *penne al pomodoro e vodka*, penne with tomato and vodka cream sauce. *Il secondo piatto*, the second course, includes three meat selections: American hamburgers ground by our Italian butcher, *scottadito d'agnello* (a petite lamb chop typical of the region), and handmade Umbrian sausages from Domenico, my favorite Italian butcher (SEE RECIPES, PAGES 88–96). All the meats are cooked on a wood-burning grill. We add sprigs of herbs to the grill to perfume the food, which results in succulent, richly flavored meats cooked to perfection.

When I serve the hamburgers, I prepare all the fixings the way we eat them at home. I arrange sliced ripe tomatoes, sweet onions, and romaine lettuce leaves on large trays for the authentic American burger. Condiments like mayonnaise, ketchup, and mustard are on the table for those brave souls who want to try a hamburger *alla Americana*. Many times, I end up giving a lesson at the table for our Italian guests on how to build a good burger. The demonstration is always great fun and much appreciated by the Italians, who find the practice amusing, if a little strange! The simple gesture of sharing iconic national foods unites our two cultures and creates a sense of conviviality.

Although our Fourth of July party is always planned in advance, a few extra guests almost always appear at the spur of the moment. These young guests are usually friends of our grown children. They're always good sports, game for anything new and culturally diverse.

At the end of the meal, I make a toast thanking the Italians for hosting us in their beautiful country. I also thank them for joining us to celebrate a holiday that means so much to us. Then there is the final toast, which goes like this: *"Un brindisi ai nostri amici italiani e l'independenza degli Stati Uniti!"*—"A toast to our Italian friends and to Independence Day!" We end the feast with sweet, sparkling wine from Veneto accompanied by Vito's Italian/American flag cake.

Our Fourth of July is a wonderful celebration of people and cultures coming together and finding common ground. On this evening in Italy, we celebrate something very special indeed: the human connection.

Bring Home a Souvenir

After spending a month in Italy, I return home with a full heart—my favorite souvenir. The old-fashioned phrase "my cup runneth over" perfectly describes my sense of inner peace. I feel good in my own skin, and I ask myself what it is about this country that makes me feel so good. Could it simply be that I'm on vacation, away from the stresses of ordinary life? Could it be that during my time in Italy I achieve what all of us long for: the ability to live in the moment? The answer lies partly in these truths. But there is something else, something far more complex, going on as well.

I have come to realize that in Italy, the business of living is not a business at all. Instead, it's an art form in which meaningful personal connections play a major part of daily existence.

To be a humane person is deeply ingrained in the Italian way of life. Generosity, empathy, and family loyalty are the cornerstones of life in Italy. In the fast-paced world where we live, many times these values are put on the back burner as we work feverishly to stay ahead. But ahead of what? Ahead of whom?

One of my main sources of well-being comes from the fact that when I'm in Italy, I'm part of a culture that values basic acts of kindness. I see this kindness when I receive help with a heavy burden after shopping in the market, or when I visit my favorite local café and am treated to a drink on the house. Simple gestures like these brighten my day. They make me feel happy and appreciated.

One aspect of the Italian culture that always amazes me is the willingness to do a favor without expectation of repayment. We have friends who are professionals—doctors, lawyers, and engineers—who have offered us counsel and medical attention, and then refuse payment for their services. This practice is all but unheard of in the United States, and a perfect illustration of Italy's great generosity and empathy.

Italy is also renowned for its sense of loyalty to family. Generations of Italians stay together. It's not unusual for multiple generations to live in the same apartment building. Family meals are a normal and essential ritual that binds the family together. Sunday *pranzo* (the midday meal) is the Italian equivalent of the Sunday supper. These meals can last from noon to early evening. They are a source of guidance, support, and love that Italians can depend on over the course of a lifetime. These gifts of the heart cannot be bought, and in Italy they are always given freely.

Upon my return from Italy, I reenter my own country with a new appreciation for the sacred in quotidian life. It is my most precious souvenir from a summer in Italy: an enlightened heart.

Adopt the Custom of *Pranzo*

Pranzo is the midday meal eaten in Italy at 1 p.m. Gathering for *pranzo* is an important ritual for all Italians. The closest tradition Americans have to *pranzo* is Sunday supper; in the United Kingdom it's afternoon tea. This meal is a diverse cultural moment in which extended family members gather to be together to eat and drink. Instating a *pranzo*-like meal in your life isn't very hard. Pick a weekend day, maybe Sunday, and make a meal that encourages the entire family to sit down together to eat their favorite foods. Start simple, creating one main dish that's well liked by everyone and add side dishes that you know will be well received. Try, if you can, to stay seasonal. These meals can be fun and don't need to be "dinner" meals. You can always do something different, like making breakfast for dinner: pancakes, eggs, bacon, and homemade biscuits with sugar butter (SEE RECIPE, PAGE 46). If you have diverse cultural roots, make a favorite recipe, like *tacos al pastor* or an Indian curry with all the condiments. Start your meal early, keeping in mind that the next day is a workday. In times past, supper was eaten early due to the farmer's schedule of early to bed, early to rise. Start the *pranzo* tradition in your own home; I guarantee that having regular family time will change your family's dynamic for the better.

Pick a weekend day, maybe Sunday, and make a meal that encourages the entire family to sit down together to eat their favorite foods.

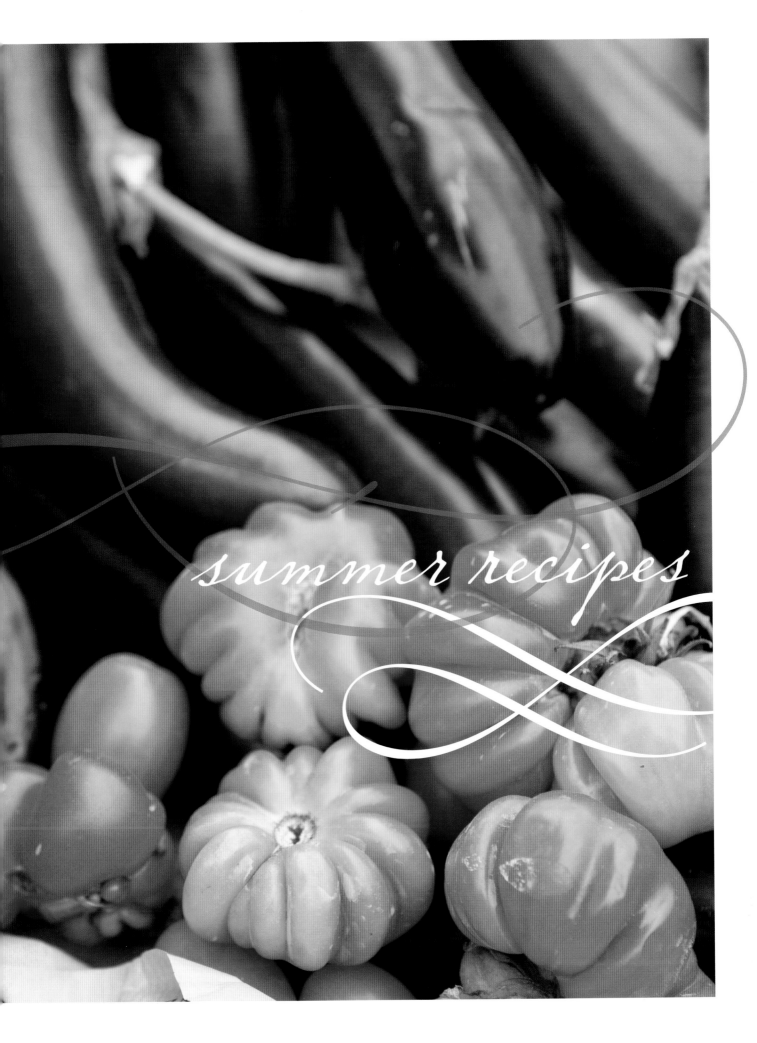

summer recipes

Daniela and Vito's Out-of-This-World Pizza Toppings

What exactly you choose to put on each pizza is completely up to you and your guests, but there are a few things you can do to make your pizzas truly extraordinary. First, use the best-quality ingredients for your toppings: homemade sauce, locally grown and preferably organic vegetables, freshly sliced cured meats, and good-quality cheeses. Second, don't be tempted to overload your pizza with too much sauce and cheese, which can result in a soggy, sloppy crust.

Sauces

Rosanna's Tomato Sauce (PAGE 172)

Extra-virgin olive oil

Cheeses

3 large balls fresh mozzarella cheese, cut into 1-inch (2.5 cm) slices

1 cup (100 g) freshly grated Parmigiano-Reggiano cheese

1 cup (100 g) freshly grated Pecorino Toscano (aged Tuscan sheep's milk cheese)

Vegetables

Zucchini, thinly sliced lengthwise, sautéed in olive oil until golden, and drained on paper towels

Yukon Gold potatoes, boiled, peeled, and cut into cubes

Eggplant, thinly sliced, grilled or sautéed in olive oil, drained on paper towels, and cut into 1-inch (2.5 cm) lengths

Small yellow onion, peeled and roasted until soft and lightly browned

1 bunch baby arugula, washed, drained, and spun dry

1 (14-ounce) (396 g) can artichoke hearts in water, drained

Meats

10 thin slices prosciutto from Parma or Norcia, Italy

15 to 25 thin slices Genoa wine salami

15 to 25 thin slices copocollo

10 thin slices pancetta (Italian unsmoked bacon)

3 mild Italian pork sausages, grilled or broiled until cooked through, then thinly sliced

Dessert toppings

1 (13-ounce) (371 g) jar Nutella (Italian chocolate hazelnut spread)

1 cup (200 g) sugar

Hamburgers alla Italiana (Hamburgers Italian Style)

I serve these hamburgers on July 4, when we host a bicultural celebration of the United States and Italy. I love these hamburgers because they have a slightly Italian twist to their flavor. I order the hamburger meat from the local Italian butcher, Domenico. This way I am assured that the meat is fresh and of good quality. He pre forms the patties for me, which makes my job so much easier. The important thing is to get the best hamburger meat and know what is in the mixture.

The secret to these hamburgers is that they are brushed with extra-virgin olive oil, lightly salted, and cooked over a wood-burning grill that has been scented with fresh rosemary and oregano. The wood fire and herbs impart a delicious flavor that makes the hamburger not just a burger, but an elegant second course for an Italian/American summer celebration.

I procure the basic hamburger buns from the local supermarket, but I toast them on the grill before serving, which gives them a toasty, smoky flavor. I serve all the fixings that we use in the States: mustard, mayo, ketchup, lettuce, and tomatoes. The guests have a choice if they want to be adventuresome and try the true American hamburger, or eat it plain, straight from the grill—the meat on its own is delicious and extremely flavorful.

Fresh rosemary and oregano sprigs

Organic hamburger meat, formed into ¼-pound (113 g) patties

Extra-virgin olive oil

Sea salt

Hamburger buns, split

Mustard

Mayonnaise

Ketchup

Lettuce

Freshly cut summer beefsteak tomatoes

Prepare a natural charcoal fire. When the coals are gray and the flames have died down, add the rosemary and oregano to the coals. Brush the hamburger patties with oil, season with salt, and grill to the desired degree of doneness. Put the buns on the grill until toasted. Serve, letting your guests choose their garnishes.

Rosanna's Tomato Vodka Sauce

SERVES 4

1 large carrot

2 ribs celery with leaves

1 onion

4 cloves garlic

½ cup (120 ml) good-quality extra-virgin olive oil

2 (28-ounce) (794 g) cans San Marzano Roma tomatoes

1 teaspoon (6 g) sea salt

½ teaspoon (2.5 g) sugar (if necessary)

¼ cup (60 ml) heavy cream

½ cup (125 ml) vodka

Pinch of pepperoncini, or hot red pepper flakes

Dice the carrot, celery, onion, and garlic (this can also be done in a food processor).

Put the oil in a large saucepan and place over medium heat. When the oil is hot, add the chopped vegetables to the pan and sauté over medium heat until just soft, about 5 minutes.

Puree the tomatoes in a food processor, then add them to the pan. Add the salt, and sugar if necessary (I find that the San Marzanos are usually sweet enough on their own). Let the sauce simmer, uncovered, for 1 hour, stirring occasionally.

Add the cream and vodka and simmer gently for 30 minutes; do not boil, or the sauce could curdle. Add the pepperoncini, then serve over pasta.

Insalata Estiva (Summer Salad)

This salad is a perfect summer dish to serve with simple pasta dressed with tomato sauce. The toasted pine nuts offer a lovely buttery, nutty flavor, not too heavy for a summer meal. The fresh mozzarella, with its soft, delicate texture, contrasts beautifully with the spicy bite of arugula to make a perfect second plate for a hot summer night.

SERVES 4 TO 6

1 bunch arugula

½ head of romaine lettuce

½ cup (60 g) pine nuts

¾ pound (340 g) fresh mozzarella in small balls

10 cherry tomatoes cut in half

¼ cup (60 ml) extra-virgin olive oil

Sea salt

Preheat the oven to 300°F (149°C) (Gas mark 2).

Wash the arugula and romaine well to remove all sand and dirt. Spin or gently pat dry and set aside in a large bowl.

Put the pine nuts on a baking sheet and toast for about 10 minutes, watching closely so they do not burn, until lightly browned. Let cool.

Add the mozzarella, pine nuts, and tomatoes to the greens and drizzle with the oil. Toss the salad so that all the ingredients are lightly coated with oil, then season lightly with salt to taste. Serve immediately.

Pasta Estiva (Summer Pasta)

Here, the soft, small mozzarella balls are cut in half so they melt sensually throughout the dish of pasta. The combination of the sweet, tangy tomato sauce with the crunchy, buttery pine nuts and soft, oozing mozzarella makes a very special eating experience.

This pasta dish is easy and inexpensive to make. It is a dish that is rich in protein and carbohydrates, making it a wonderful one-dish meal. A simple green salad or crudités (raw cut-up vegetables) with small bowls of extra-virgin olive oil and sea salt for dipping served alongside is perfect, and a crisp dry white wine like a Greghetto or a Pinot Grigio makes the meal complete.

SERVES 4 TO 6

¼ cup (60 ml) extra-virgin olive oil

1 pound (454 g) cherry tomatoes, halved

10 fresh basil leaves, roughly chopped, plus more whole leaves for garnish

1 clove garlic, minced

1 pound (454 g) dried short pasta (such as penne or campanelle)

15 small balls fresh mozzarella, halved

¼ cup (30 g) pine nuts, toasted (SEE PAGE 90)

½ teaspoon (2.5 g) sea salt

In a large sauté pan, heat the oil over medium heat. Add the tomatoes, basil, and garlic.

Cook until the tomatoes are soft, 15 to 20 minutes. Remove from the heat.

Cook the pasta in a large pot of boiling salted water until al dente; drain well, then transfer the pasta to the sauté pan with the sauce. Add the mozzarella balls and toss to combine them with the tomato sauce and pasta. Add the pine nuts and toss. Add the salt and mix again. Serve immediately on a large oval platter, garnished with large basil leaves.

Ivana's Pasta alla Norcina

This delicious pasta was shared with me by a wonderful cook from Assisi, Italy. Ivana uses only the freshest local ingredients. She brings me zucchini from her garden, duck sauce from ducks she has raised on her farm, and delicious *torta la testo*, a wonderful flatbread eaten in Umbria with prosciutto. Pasta alla Norcina is a rich, earthy dish that celebrates the summer truffle that is found in the woods surrounding the hills of Umbria. The Umbrian truffle is unparalleled in its luscious, deep aroma and taste. This dish is slightly expensive due to the cost of the truffles, but it is a one-dish meal that needs only a light green salad made with arugula and romaine lettuce as an accompaniment.

SERVES 4

⅓ cup (75 ml) extra-virgin olive oil

2 large links pork sausage, casings removed

1 clove garlic, minced

1 anchovy, chopped

½ cup (125 ml) dry white wine

½ cup (118 ml) heavy cream

1¾ ounces (50 g) black truffles (SEE NOTE)

1 pound (454 g) dried penne pasta, preferably
De Cecco brand

Sea salt

In a large sauté pan, heat the oil over medium heat. Add the sausage, garlic, and anchovy and cook, stirring frequently, until the sausage is thoroughly cooked, about 15 minutes. The meat should be tan, with no pink remaining.

Add the wine and cook until it's almost evaporated. Add the cream and cook over low heat until the sauce is thickened slightly, about 10 minutes.

Using a small grater, grate the truffle over the sauce, reserving a bit of the truffle for garnish and making sure to scrape the back of the grater to get all the truffle into the sauce. (Alternatively, shave the truffles into paper-thin slices.)

Meanwhile, cook the pasta in a large pot of boiling salted water until al dente; drain well, then transfer the pasta to the sauté pan with the sauce. Toss to coat the pasta with the sauce. Add salt to taste, then spoon the pasta into individual serving bowls and grate more truffle over the top. Serve immediately.

NOTE: *You can find bottled black truffles in gourmet stores or on the Internet.*

Scottadito d'Agnello
(Burn Your Fingers Lamb)

This is a difficult recipe to replicate outside of Italy, as I've had a hard time finding the right cut of lamb. The closest I have come to achieving the flavorful simplicity of this dish is by purchasing a rack of lamb and having the butcher cut the rack into individual chops. A rack of lamb is quite expensive, so another alternative is lamb chops cut to about 1 inch (2.5 cm) thick by the butcher.

This dish requires very little preparation: With good meat, a garlic clove, fresh rosemary, and the best extra-virgin olive oil, it has all the flavor you could ever want. Lamb can sometimes taste a little gamey, but in this dish it's tamed by the herbs and olive oil. Use your hands while eating the chops—as we all know, the best meat is that which is right next to the bone. Serve them with a simple romaine lettuce salad with Francesca's Favorite Salad Dressing (PAGE 168), or Insalata Estiva (PAGE 90).

SERVES 4

12 to 16 lamb chops (3 or 4 per person)

1 clove garlic, halved

Extra-virgin olive oil

3 sprigs fresh rosemary, stemmed and chopped, plus more whole sprigs for the fire if desired

Sea salt

Rub the chops on both sides with the cut garlic, then drizzle lightly with oil and sprinkle with the chopped rosemary. Season liberally with salt.

If you are using a wood or charcoal fire, add a few sprigs of rosemary to the coals after they turn gray. Cook the chops, turning once, until cooked to the desired degree of doneness. If you are using a broiler, preheat it to high. Arrange the lamb chops in one layer on a rimmed baking sheet or broiler pan. Broil for about 5 minutes on each side, until cooked to the desired degree of doneness. Serve immediately.

Delicately Thin Pork Chops,
with Extra-Virgin Olive Oil and
Fresh Oregano

One custom I love about Italy is the small portions of meat they serve as a second course. Ask your butcher to cut the pork chops to about ½-inch (1.3 cm) thick, with the bone left in. The chops are baked in the oven, and because they are so thin it takes no time at all. The simplicity of Italian cooking is that the true flavors of the food shine through, as is the case with these delicious pork chops seasoned only with oregano, salt, and olive oil. Serve them with Insalata Estiva (PAGE 90).

SERVES 4 TO 6

6 (½-inch-thick) (1.3 cm) pork chops

Extra-virgin olive oil

1 bunch fresh oregano, chopped

Sea salt

Preheat the oven to 350°F (177°C) (Gas mark 4).

Arrange the pork chops on a rimmed baking sheet. Drizzle lightly with oil. Sprinkle the oregano over the chops and season with salt to taste. Bake for about 20 minutes, until the pink at the center is just gone; be careful to not overcook them or the chops will be dry. Serve immediately.

Ricotta Tart

This simple, classic tart from central and southern Italy is similar to a cheesecake, but fluffy and light, and without the heavy flavor and feel of cream cheese. A slice of this tart makes a perfect after-dinner dessert during the summer or an ideal midday snack.

MAKES 1 (9-INCH TART) (23 CM); SERVES 6 TO 8

2 cups (270 g) part-skim ricotta

3 large eggs

1 cup (200 g) sugar

½ cup (125ml) whipping cream

Grated zest of 1 lemon

½ cup (125 ml) whole milk

½ recipe (1 ball) My Mom's Extra-Flaky Pie Crust Dough (PAGE 138)

Preheat the oven to 350°F (177°C) (Gas mark 4).

In a large bowl, combine the ricotta, eggs, sugar, cream, lemon zest, and milk. Set aside in the refrigerator.

On a pastry cloth, using a floured rolling pin covered with a pastry stocking, roll the dough out into an 11-inch (28 cm) circle. Slip a pie pan under the dough and gently adjust it to fit a 9-inch tart pan. Use your knuckle to form a fluted edge around the pie. Fill with the ricotta mixture. Bake for about 50 minutes, until a knife inserted into the filling in the center of the tart comes out clean and the crust is browned.

Caffè Scherato ("Shakerato")

This is the summer drink in Italy, and one of my favorite obsessions during the summer months. It's like having a velvety blended coffee with an adult icy feel. It is luscious and decadent and will give you the get-up-and-go energy needed on a hot day. I love this drink and am clearly addicted to its out-of-this-world combination of flavors and play of blended ice and *la crema* of the espresso. For this drink, I prefer espresso brewed from Starbucks Italian Roast coffee, which is dark and rich enough to stand up to the ice.

In Italy it is served in champagne flutes or wineglasses—an elegant and hip way to drink coffee. After all, *la bella figura* (making a good impression) is what it is all about in Italy. Enjoy a bit of *la dolce vita* and indulge in this delicious summer drink.

SERVES 1

2 shots freshly brewed espresso

1 tablespoon simple syrup (14 ml) or honey (21 g)

2 to 4 ice cubes

Cocoa powder

Put the espresso, simple syrup, and ice in a blender and blend until you get a frothy texture. Pour into a wineglass or champagne flute. Dust with cocoa powder and enjoy a sensual, tasty treat.

Iced Caffè Latte

I love the pick-me-up that coffee gives me; when the sun is hot and saps me of my energy, there is nothing more appealing than a cool iced caffè latte flavored with honey or simple syrup. I like Starbucks Italian Roast or Sumatra coffee here. If you're using an espresso maker, grind the coffee very fine; if using a French press, grind it coarse. Iced coffee like this is best served in a tall tumbler that feels good in your hand, like our Rosanna recycled Mexican glass tumbler.

SERVES 1

**1 cup freshly brewed espresso,
or 1 small pot coffee made in a French press**

2% milk

½ teaspoon simple syrup (2.5 ml) or honey (3.5 g)

3 ice cubes

Put the coffee in a porcelain pitcher in the refrigerator until well chilled.

Fill a tumbler halfway with milk. Add the simple syrup and stir well. Add the ice and fill the glass with coffee; stir well.

fall

Transition gracefully.

In France, there is a special term for the transition from summer vacation to fall and the beginning of school and all the changes—physical and psychological— that come about after a long, lazy summer. The French call this period *la rentrée scolaire*. Although *la rentrée* revolves around the end of the children's summer holiday and the beginning of a new school year, the phrase refers to much more than the season when classes resume. Traditionally, businesses in France and much of the rest of Europe (even, in recent years, in the U.K.) essentially shut their doors during the month of August (and a good part of July). Employees say their goodbyes in midsummer, and tasks that can wait are put on hold until *après la rentrée*—and, really, what is so important that it can't wait until the weather cools off a bit?

Parents and children return from extended vacations only reluctantly, sporting golden tans developed over the course of a long, carefree summer, resigned to the fact that it's time to reenter the world of responsibility and adhere to the structured schedules of school and work. This can be a rude awakening, and, no matter that it happens every year, the abrupt change in season never fails to prompt a cascade of shoulder shrugs and ooh la la's across France.

Although Americans don't tend to take weeks-long summer vacations, and so don't have a well-established reentry ritual like the French, we too might feel the bittersweet longing for the dog days of summer as Labor Day looms nearer. I admit that, as much as I enjoy fall after it arrives, I squeeze summer to the last drop.

To prolong the feeling of summer as long as possible, I have a few tricks. One is denial; instead of spending the last days before school starts anxious about the fast-approaching end of the holiday, I simply pretend I have much more time before my girls begin school again than I actually do. Denial can be a beautiful thing. The older I get, the more I see how a little innocent suspension of reality can be a wonderful way to sustain happiness.

If you too are a lover of summer and tend to experience a certain melancholy as the season draws to a close, here are a few ways to make the most of its last days. Buy and organize all school supplies as soon as you receive instructions from your child's new teacher (this way you and yours won't have to worry about checking everything off the list at the last minute, and can enjoy, say, one last day at the pool). Purchase new school clothes, whether they will be wearing uniforms or free dress, weeks before the first day back to school. This way the focus can stay on the last days of summer and your children will be free to enjoy the amazing pre–Labor Day weather. Make sure you don't overschedule yourselves or your children. Be in the moment and make the most of it!

Even if you do wait until the last minute, make the school-supply outing into an expedition to prepare your children as they embark on a new scholastic adventure. Emphasize the exciting parts of starting a new school year. A new backpack, lunch box, or school binder can be a fun purchase because they provide a creative outlet for your child to express his or her unique personality and tastes. Remind your kids how delighted they'll be to reunite with old friends after the long summer. Position your children for the new world that a new grade level will open up to them. For example, you could say, "Won't it be interesting to learn about the jungles of South America this year? Did you know that more than a thousand species of bugs live in tropical rainforests?" Prepare them for the wonders they'll be learning and experiencing. Prepping your children for an engaging, interesting year will make the transition easier and give them a head start on the intellectual journey they're about to embark upon.

The beginning of the school year still affords small windows of opportunity to take mini-breaks or day trips with your family. If you can, try to schedule some special time to visit a favorite place that will give you that last "hit" of summer. These mini-vacations renew the spirit and help us keep our families united before the mad dash of fall activities, and they create memories of well-being for us to draw upon during the hectic months ahead. For our last shot of summer, my family goes to the Oregon coast. We pick wild blackberries and make pies to deliver to our neighbors. It may seem a little hokey, but it's our way of connecting to a community we see far too infrequently. It's a lovely way to end the summer and begin the fall with grace and ease. Remember, summer doesn't officially end until September 22. Enjoy every moment you have left.

Spend Time with College-Age Kids

Trying to get your college-age kids to stay home is no small feat. I would say it's next to impossible unless you're willing to make some concessions. Once your child leaves for college, the way you interact will change. When they come home to visit, during the school year or over the summers, you'll have to alter your expectations of how they spend their time. Over the past two years I've learned a lot about what I can do to engage with my college-age daughter while she's home.

First, and probably most importantly, have a good supply of tasty food at home. After nine months of living in cramped dorms and eating cafeteria food, college students are starving for home-cooked meals. Rising to the occasion can be a daunting task, especially if your child has turned vegetarian or vegan. My daughter left for college and came back a vegetarian, so I always stock the refrigerator with lots of organic fruits and vegetables and the pantry with a variety of beans and nuts. I plan alluring menus featuring her favorite dishes that she hasn't been able to eat while she was away.

For many young adults coming home from college, sharing cooking duties transforms from a chore into a fun and entertaining activity. Many nights, I've returned to a wonderful dinner my daughter has prepared for the family on her own. After years of cooking for my family, it's a great treat to come home to a delicious meal after a hard day of work. I'm proud of my daughter's abilities and delighted to be relieved of cooking for the evening.

To make those home-cooked meals even more enticing, have lots of good music that crosses the generation barrier. Try introducing some music that was part of your generation. For example, I love the Beatles, the Rolling Stones, the Grateful Dead, Marvin Gaye, Al Green, Aretha Franklin, and, dare I say, Burt Bacharach. I am always surprised how my daughter loves my music. On the other hand, also be open to listening to your children's music. You too might discover some surprisingly enjoyable contemporary music. Ask your children what their favorites are and invite them to play it while they are at home.

After experiencing the all-encompassing stimulation of university life, family time can seem a little lackluster by comparison. To make home more attractive to an energetic young adult, I try to cultivate a relaxed *que sera sera* environment, and I encourage my daughter to

bring her friends home. Some nights, sleepovers fill every possible bedroom space. I wake to find sleeping bags and makeshift couch-cushion mattresses strewn throughout every room in the house. Music playing loudly in the background and kids lounging on every available surface—it feels like the '70s all over again, and I am magically transported back to my own youth. I love the young energy that pervades the house. I am also privy to some pretty interesting conversations, which give me a quick lesson on what's happening in this new generation and the influences that are shaping our children's futures.

On sleepover mornings, I cook a delicious breakfast, careful to navigate the special diets of our guests. (SPONTANEOUS GET-TOGETHERS LIKE THESE ARE ONE OF MANY REASONS IT'S IMPORTANT TO HAVE A WELL-STOCKED PANTRY; SEE PAGE 68) As chaotic as these gatherings can be, I relish them as an opportunity to once again become an active participant in my daughter's life and, inspired by her exuberance, to rediscover my own enthusiasm as well.

After my eldest daughter departs for college, I'm left with a wonderful buffer to empty-nest loneliness: my twelve-year-old daughter. A younger child's needs are completely different from those of a young adult, and I find this other set of requirements charming and heart-warming. Taking care of a "little one" allows me to cling to my role as full-time mom versus a Christmas/spring-break mom a bit longer.

Movie Night with the Girls:
Never Refuse an Invitation to Hang Out

One evening, my daughter and her friends invited me along to a late-night movie. I balked, saying I could never stay up that late. "Come on, Mom, it'll be fun!" my daughter said as she handed me a cup of espresso. I downed the shot, and before I knew it was out the door on the way to the movies. When we arrived at the theater we were greeted by a large group of lovely twenty-year-old women. And my daughter was right; it was great fun.

As we walked out of the theater, those twenty-year-olds were greeted by a group of young men who happened to be passing by. Much to my embarrassment, but not surprisingly, they became interested in the group of beautiful young women. My three extra decades of life experience inspired me to duck into a doorway to watch the scene play out in front of me. I enjoyed watching the interactions among these smart women and men as much as I'd enjoyed the movie, even if it was from behind a pair of Ray-Bans on a dark night.

If you're fortunate enough to be invited on an outing by your children, by all means go. It's an exciting experience to be a part of this new world, even if just for an evening. Observe and enjoy your child as a young adult. You might learn something about yourself and the new generation emerging.

Extend Childhood

I find that one of the biggest challenges of rearing an elementary- or middle-school-age child in today's world is figuring out how to slow down the breakneck speed of the back-to-school transition. Everything is amped up. Children are immediately enrolled in activities and have a heavy homework load as early as the first week of school. I'm constantly looking for ways to slow things down and allow my daughter to be a "little girl," unburdened by stress, for as long as possible.

Prolong your children's childhood. Don't push them to grow up before their time. I believe that the longer the childhood, the healthier the child. Let the end of summer guide you, and provide a way to slowly prepare them for reentry into the scholastic year. Schedule short vacations to nearby spots before school starts. Local parks, lakes, rivers, beaches, or mountains make ideal day trips or weekend getaways to make the most of the last days of summer. Get close to nature and soak in every last bit of the golden rays of the sun.

I remember carefree afternoons spent in unstructured play as one of the best parts of my childhood because the magic of that time in one's life is based on an ability to play creatively. During the summer, unfettered by homework and after-school commitments, the imagination takes center stage. I purposely avoid scheduling "play dates" in advance, and instead let them happen naturally. If my daughter wants company, we simply pick up the phone and see who's around. Luckily, one of her closest friends lives across the street. This is one way I try to revive the bygone tradition of spontaneous play and unstructured free time.

To encourage play that doesn't involve computers or electronic devices, I keep a large closet stocked with old clothes and costumes from my older daughter's theater days for dress-up. I also have an open kitchen, and I invite the children to cook when they feel like it. A real childhood, rather than a never-ending preparation for adulthood, is the greatest gift we can give our children. Childhood is a time in life to protect and nurture. Encourage kids to slow down. They have their whole lives to be adults. For the time being, let your children be children.

Slow Down with a Trip to the Country

One way to break up the hectic days of fall, with its busy schedules of school activities, sports events, parties, work, and homework, is a Saturday drive to a nearby orchard for apple picking or nut gathering. As young girls, my sisters and I would accompany our mother each fall to the orchards around Portland, Oregon, where we loaded baskets full of the sweet, crisp fresh apples the Pacific Northwest is known for. Mother would make them into applesauce—canned for use throughout the year, of course—and they'd appear all winter in her comforting baked apple dumplings and famous apple pies. Most varieties of apple store very well, and fresh, delicate slices would find their way from the cool larder in our garage into most of our packed lunches.

Another favorite of my mother's were the delicious nuts grown in Oregon. There are those who love nuts and those who don't. We were nut people. There were always huge bowls full of multiple varieties of nuts and crackers ready for easy snacking. A vegan's paradise, Oregon offers a mind-boggling assortment of these delicious and vitamin-rich foods. Hazelnuts are grown here in great quantities, making Oregon one of the top exporters in the world. English walnuts and chestnuts were also sought out by my mother in the fall.

Gathering food from the countryside can be difficult in these busy times, but I believe that if we make the choice to make quality foods a part of our lives, the ritual of harvesting can be integrated into our routine. To be in touch with nature ensures us a food supply that will truly nourish our bodies and keep us connected to the earth.

Pack small thermal containers for hot meals. Warm up leftovers in the morning, and they'll stay hot until lunchtime. Keep small bags of blue gel ice in the freezer and pack one in with cold lunches to keep them fresh and safe.

Make Bag Lunches Fresh and Delicious

With so little time and so much to accomplish, it's difficult to do everything that we'd like to do in caring for our children. If we could, many of us would cook every meal for them ourselves, from scratch, take educational vacations, and spend our free evenings reading and discussing the classics. Obviously this isn't even remotely possible (or desirable), but there's one very basic thing we should try to do as often as possible: prepare food that is healthy and nutritious. Feeding our children well is the most important thing we can do to ensure they lead healthy lives later on. Packing homemade lunches will establish good eating habits that will last a lifetime. Making lunch every day—before lunchtime, no less—can seem like a daunting task, as it adds one more thing to our morning to-do lists, but eating a good lunch is so important for a growing child that the effort involved comes to seem negligible. Far better than letting them fend for themselves in the cafeteria lunch line, sending our kids to school with a well-balanced meal ready to eat allows us to show them, by example, how to eat healthfully. They'll carry that experience with them when they leave home to navigate the world of food on their own.

Every Sunday evening, I roast half an organic turkey for a week of school lunches. Turkey is a light, healthful protein perfect for sandwiches. Try fresh roasted turkey on sourdough, with thinly sliced Granny Smith apple, a thin smear of brie or a slice of Swiss cheese, and a sprinkle of freshly ground black pepper. Or turkey with a thin spread of tart berry jam on dark whole-grain bread. Make turkey salad with the smaller bits at the end of the week—add a few pinches of curry powder and some raisins for a retro version.

Reheated pasta or homemade soup can go into a small stainless-steel Thermos for a hot lunch. I also keep a supply of healthy treats like granola bars, raisins, and organic crackers on hand. The vegetable bin in the refrigerator is always filled with organic baby carrots, celery, and Washington State organic apples.

A healthy lunch says "I love you" in so many ways. For my twelve-year-old, it's a reminder during the school day that I'm there with her. After all, food is love. What better way to express care than by preparing a homemade lunch that is full of good food?

Embrace Sports as a Lesson in Living

Throughout their childhoods, both of my daughters played sports. Soccer, basketball, volleyball—whatever was in season, they played it. As part of a generation whose girls were not encouraged to be athletes, this was an adjustment for me.

When my first daughter's inaugural soccer season began, I was lost. I didn't know the game or the terms, and I went to my first daughter's matches reluctantly. Each was scheduled for as early as possible on Saturday mornings at some far-off field that took forever to find. The fall weather was inevitably rainy and cold, and those two miserable hours always ended with a sick little girl. Or so it seemed.

Then my second daughter began to play. By this time I'd learned the rules, and I found myself actually looking forward to the events as opportunities to connect with the other team parents. These gatherings helped me to feel a part of a community of like-minded parents. Together we cheered our daughters to victory and comforted and encouraged them when they lost. And as if by magic, everything I thought had been out of my control changed. The match locations were closer to home, the weather was wonderful, and my daughter never got sick after a rainy game. Interesting what a change in attitude can do!

The importance of teamwork, having tenacity in difficult circumstances, and a feeling of self-worth were only some of the valuable life lessons the girls learned during their time on the field and on the court. I'm so pleased that my daughters are growing up in a society that doesn't bar them from certain activities because they are female. I revel in their triumphs and

defeats, knowing they're learning invaluable lessons either way. I come away from those games inspired and motivated, knowing their futures will be bright.

Children's sports activities are an important part of a child's education. They teach the child teamwork, discipline, and how to build solid relationships with other teammates and coaches. There is always some type of team sport available during the year. Encourage your children to at least try a sport; no matter how athletically inclined they are, they will surely benefit from the experience of being part of a team and working toward a goal together, building a strong sense of what lies ahead for them in the adult world. Sports involvement is particularly beneficial to young women, as it can provide them with a feeling of empowerment and self-esteem.

Mark the Passage of Time

Fall is a time that brings profound change. Summer is over, and a new way of living begins. Responsibilities loom before us, our workload increases, separation from our children leaves us lonely, and our natural world tells us it's time to snap to and prepare for winter. Even though these transitions can be disconcerting, there is great beauty in this change. Change makes us recognize that we are alive and active participants in our world. It shakes us up. It says, "Pay attention! The world is changing, and so are you." During the change in seasons, we have the opportunity for introspection and personal growth. All we have to do is key in to nature's rhythm and go with the flow. I see this change as nature's way of preparing us for growth and for maturity of the spirit.

Appreciate Nature's Transformations

As summer gradually, slowly transitions to winter over the course of several months, the quality of the air changes and we can see and feel nature shedding its fruits, preparing for the barren season. In the fall the quality of the natural light takes on a golden glow, a deep burnt umber color that reflects the sun's changing position in the sky, and an aura of mystery and magic takes over. It's time to light candles around the house, creating an atmosphere of warmth and comfort to ward off the coming chill.

People have paid attention to the cycles of nature since the beginnings of civilization. Listen to your inner voice, and your natural intuitions. These drives are the ways collective human history speaks to us. Celebrations like Halloween have ancient origins dating back two thousand years, to the Celts. Fall rituals that celebrate the end of the harvest are an important part of preparing for the challenges of the cold season.

The home is the center of life. It is a place to gather strength. It is at home that we can create an atmosphere of sustained comfort and tradition. Late fall is the perfect time to prepare the home for what lies ahead. Preserves have been put up, root vegetables are going into cold storage, the harvest is finished. As winter approaches and we weatherproof our lives, old-fashioned phrases like "hunkering down" take on special meaning.

Let fall be the signal for us to change our attitude toward the work we do and how we approach life. Fall signifies the maturation of nature, and it is also a time to shed the carefree attitude of summer and embrace the oncoming responsibilities of late fall and winter.

Cook more, and prepare for the ensuing cold months. Prepare extra pasta sauces and soups, and freeze the last bounty of the season for a rich and well-stocked pantry and freezer. Fill the freezer with fruits, vegetables, and anything that won't be available during the winter as insurance that you will eat healthily and well during the winter months.

Celebrate Halloween with Verve and Enthusiasm

Even if you aren't one of those people who start working on next year's Halloween costumes on November 1, it's fun to plan ahead for the most delightful holiday of the season.

At least a week before Halloween, start going through your closets to find interesting clothes that can be fashioned into a costume. If you have small children, scour the local thrift stores to find interesting costumes that will fit small bodies. Brainstorm with your kids about what theme they would be excited about exploring. Read about what is happening culturally and in the movies. These are good places to start your search for an innovative costume. Follow the same rule for adult costumes.

Try on everything in advance. Critique one another to see what you can add to make the costume really tell a story. Use makeup and props from around the house to achieve the right look. Have everything planned in advance, so there is no last-minute scrambling.

A few days before Halloween, bake Halloween-themed treats to offer guests and family on the special day. Cupcakes with pumpkin and cat faces (SEE RECIPE, PAGE 143) can be stored at room temperature for several days if they're put in tins to ensure freshness. Serve them on the day of Halloween, on shiny black cake pedestals. The delicious vanilla and chocolate owl cookies with chocolate chips for eyes and a salty cashew for a nose (SEE RECIPE, PAGE 140) will also keep well so they can be prepared in advance. Involve your children in the baking and assembly of the cookies. Doing this a few days before Halloween is a fun and creative activity that will get everyone in the mood for the big day.

Carve the pumpkins just before October 31 so they don't become moldy and collapse— unless that's the look you want. Three days is a good window of time to ensure fresh, crisp pumpkins that will hold up through Halloween evening.

Ten Steps to Successful Pumpkin Carving

1. Pick out pumpkins that are shaped well for carving, whether you prefer smooth globes for happy faces or misshapen blobs for more monstrous visages.

2. Spread out old newspapers on a big table or on the floor and get ready to carve.

3. Have the following items handy:

   - Large bowls for the pulp.

   - Small bowls for saving the seeds.

   - Large serving spoons for scooping out the insides of the pumpkins.

   - Carving tools: Specialized pumpkin-carving instruments are great for safe and creative cutting—they include various gougers, scoops, knives, and saws that can be used to achieve interesting effects. If your kids are old enough to use them, invest in at least two sets, so you and your children can carve simultaneously. Of course, you can always just use regular kitchen utensils.

   - Paper towels for wiping hands and cleaning off the face of the pumpkin prior to drawing the design on the face.

   - Felt-tip pen for drawing the design on the pumpkin, plus scrap paper for sketching the design beforehand.

   - Candles (3-by-3-inch pillars are best because they're sturdy and less prone to tipping than narrower ones) or battery-operated lights to put inside the pumpkins when you're finished.

4. Draw a circle around the top that you will cut to open the pumpkin, making sure it is big enough to reach inside to clean the pumpkin. Alternatively, cut a hole in the bottom of the pumpkin; that way, you can easily light a candle in a candle holder or on a plate, then carefully lower the carved pumpkin over the candle—avoiding the timeless annoyance of lighting a candle through the top of the gourd.

5. Clean out the insides of the pumpkin thoroughly, taking out the pulp and separating the pulp from the seeds. Save the seeds for cleaning later and then roasting for a delicious fall snack (see recipe, page 128).

6. Pick the side of the pumpkin that has the most personality. Sometimes dimples and imperfections on a pumpkin's face can add real character and individuality to a jack-o'-lantern.

7. Sketch out the design of the face on a sheet of paper, then use a black felt-tip pen to copy the design directly onto the pumpkin.

8. Carve cautiously. Even if your child is mature enough to carve on her own, make sure to watch closely. If you have younger children, let them be the scoopers and the separators of the seed and the pulp (they'll have a grand time with the goop and gore), or put them in charge of drawing the design on the paper.

9. When carved, place your pumpkins outside near your front door. Make sure they are not exposed to the rain or other elements, which could cause them to mold and break down more quickly. I use stools, benches, and small wooden foot rests to make different levels of display. If you have stairs that lead up to your home, place a pumpkin or two on each stair leading to your front door.

10. Clean up the mess. Have a large plastic garbage bag nearby to throw all the pulp and discarded shards of pumpkin into. Save the bowl of seeds and take them to the kitchen.

Don't Stop with the Pumpkin

There are so many ways to decorate for Halloween beyond putting a jack-o'-lantern on the stoop. Let your own personality and interests be your guides in how you decide to decorate. Take your time and don't rush the decorating process, which for me is almost as much fun as the holiday itself. If the pumpkin carving takes up too much time for one evening, decorate the house on another night; enlist your kids to help after school before homework begins. Here are a few ideas for Halloween decorating themes.

Use fall and the beauty of the natural world to inspire your decorations. Select beautiful squashes, gourds, and fall leaves to adorn your home. Haystacks, kindly scarecrows, and lush fall wreaths can also be incorporated into this theme. Use warm earth tones in the fabrics you choose, perhaps accented with one bright complementary color for contrast.

The Mexican Day of the Dead, or El Día de los Muertos—which is actually celebrated over two days, November 1 and 2—is a rich source of ideas for Halloween decorations. Look at pictures of the festival online for inspiration, then go to a local Mexican import store to find the small figures of skeletons, or *calacas*, that are used during the celebration in Mexico. Arrange your collection of *calacas* on an antique tray, interspersed with small votive candles to create an ambiance of mystery. Add Christian crosses, bunches of the traditional marigolds, and anything skull-shaped.

You could also, of course, simply make your house as scary as possible. Purchase or make frightening figures like skeletons, witches, ghouls, monsters, ravens, bats, and anything dark and foreboding. Use lots of votives, hurricane candles, and black candlesticks to set the mood for a gothic atmosphere. Faux spiderwebs, crooked tombstones, skulls, and, for the slightly more ambitious decorators among us, dry ice would not be out of place here.

At the very least, decorate your doorstep so that trick-or-treaters will stop by. Make them feel welcome (if pleasantly scared, depending on how you decided to decorate), and be sure to remove any hazards or obstructions that might keep them from approaching your house—it helps to have the doorway, and walkway if you have one, well lit. Even if you don't have kids at home, decorate as if you do!

Make the Children's Halloween Night Special

Whatever your theme for the evening, set a small table (such as a TV tray) near the front door and drape it with a black cloth or a Halloween-themed tablecloth. Place a bowl on the table and fill it with various candies and treats. If you have children, have them help you select the candy. They know what candy is "cool" and highly sought after by their peers. If in doubt, go with chocolate, but be sure to offer a selection of candies, and possibly a few "healthier" options for the kids with stricter parents. It hardly needs saying anymore, but be sure the candies are individually wrapped in their original commercial packaging so that kids and parents know they're safe. You will be delighted by the "oohs" and "ahhs" that the bowl of candy will produce when the doorbell rings and the children are presented with their treat.

On Halloween night, before the kids set off on their trick-or-treating adventures, make a dinner that is easy to prepare, like a lentil soup with crusty bread (SEE RECIPE, PAGE 131), and hearty enough to warm the tummies of the children before the big night.

When the children come home, help them sort through their candy. Discard anything that is opened or that looks suspicious. Help them sort the candy by type and flavor. It is really fun for younger kids to sort and arrange their loot so that they can appreciate what they have collected. Have an old shoebox ready for them to begin arranging by type: all chocolate candies are in one corner, all fruit candies in another, and so on. When the box

is filled it is a wonderful way for them to see the goodies they can look forward to eating and sharing. You might want to make a rule about how many they are allowed per week. I give my daughter permission to eat whatever she wants on Halloween night—it's her reward for all her "hard work" trick-or-treating and a way to celebrate the last few hours of a joyful holiday. The pure, innocent pleasure of a child's Halloween only lasts a short time before childhood is over. Let her enjoy it.

Halloween Tricks and Treats for Adults

Celebrate the holiday even if you have no children at home. On Halloween night, stage an adult dinner party

trick-or-treaters (remember to turn on the porch light). Rent your movie ahead of time, as the classic horror flicks are difficult to find when Halloween approaches. The 1963 version of *The Haunting*, directed by Robert Wise and starring Julie Harris, is a great psychological thriller, and the 1979 version of *Dracula* (my favorite) stars Frank Langella as the sexiest Dracula you will ever see, in a jewel of a film. Choose some classical music to play when you're not viewing the movie. The "Dies Irae" of Mozart's *Requiem* is appropriately spooky, as is "*O Fortuna*" from the *Carmina Burana* by Carl Orff. Bach's *Toccata and Fugue* is the perfect mood-setting music if you want to create the feeling of a haunted house. Set the table with black dishes, and make sure there are lots of candlesticks—preferably black tapers and pillars and small votives to create a gothic look.

Serve a variety of foods that can be easily enjoyed during the movie. Set out a selection of cheeses on a rustic cutting board. Fill bowls with salted nuts—making sure you have plenty of the favorites: cashews, almonds, and Spanish peanuts—and Italian wine-cured olives and French black olives marinated in thyme or garlic. Serve a big hunk of Parmigiano-Reggiano cheese on a wood cutting board along with a bowl or basket of crunchy flatbreads and slices of hand-formed European breads. Offer a big platter of antipasto or sliced Italian cold cuts like proscuitto, salami, and capocollo. Drink a really great blood-red wine like a Barolo or Amarone. There is no better way to celebrate Halloween as an adult.

that sets the produce and bounty of the season as the centerpiece of the celebration. Serve baked squash, hearty roast chicken with porcini mushrooms (SEE RECIPES, PAGES 128 AND 167), wild rice, and a delicious Amarone, a red wine from Italy. Choose a multicultural theme for your decorations, whether it's the Mexican Day of the Dead, the Celtic All Hallows Eve, or the Christian All Saints' Day. Infuse your home with the symbols that represent the harvest and the maturity that nature is spilling forth for us all to enjoy.

For a less formal get-together, invite your friends over on Halloween to watch a classic scary movie and enjoy great finger foods while you greet the

Be Grateful and Generous

Every agrarian (or formerly agrarian) culture has some version of the celebration of the harvest, an important seasonal marker throughout the world. The county fairs popular throughout the United States have their roots in the ancient European post-harvest markets that still occur today. The Chinese and Vietnamese celebrate the Autumn Moon Festival in mid- or late September (naturally, the dates are set each year by the phases of the moon), a time when farmers can relax after the harvest ends. Fall trees are planted, mooncakes are consumed under the bright glow of their namesake, lovers unite, and paper lanterns illuminate the streets

at night. Koreans have Chusok—also known as Korean Thanksgiving, which apart from the food served (the traditional food being not roast turkey but rice cakes steamed over pine needles) is remarkably similar in spirit to the American version. The Jewish holiday Sukkot not only celebrates the harvest but serves as a remembrance of the ancient Jews who wandered the Middle East living in huts (*sukkahs*) on their way to the Holy Land. During the weeklong holiday, families take their meals in makeshift *sukkahs* under the stars. The vernal equinox, the day in late September when the periods of light and dark are of equal length, is a special day for Buddhists, for whom it symbolizes the equality of all things.

American Thanksgiving is a time to celebrate the beginnings of the nation, but it's also a time to be thankful for the bounty nature brings forth for our sustenance and enjoyment, to pay homage to the gradual passage from fall to winter. Marking the transition in some way is an important part of being an active member of humanity, as you're presented with an opportunity to reach out to family and friends and to be grateful for what nature has bestowed upon us. It is also, perhaps most importantly, a time to share, to open our hearts, to be generous as well as thankful for the generosity of others.

Serve a Memorable Thanksgiving Meal

For most Americans, Thanksgiving dinner centers around a turkey. Choose an organic local bird, preferably free-range (that is, not caged). The flavor will be more

interesting than the usual frozen grocery-store varieties. Make a paste of fresh herbs, olive oil, and garlic and rub it under the turkey's skin the day before Thanksgiving; this will make the meat succulent and juicy.

For sides, take your cue from the delicious variety of fall vegetables available in your local market and roast them in the oven as the turkey cooks, with extra-virgin olive oil, sea salt, and fresh rosemary and sage (SEE RECIPE, PAGE 126). Cook local squash instead of sweet potatoes, if you'd like a change of pace (SEE RECIPE, PAGE 128). Add a dish to your Thanksgiving table that is distinctly yours; it could be from another food culture than your own—as long as you can offer the basics that your family will tend to expect, feel free to get creative.

Instead of pumpkin pie, make a fruit pie or a fruit cobbler from crisp Washington State apples or a local crop. Apple dumplings (SEE RECIPE, PAGE 132) are a fun and informal fall dessert served with vanilla ice cream.

Gingerbread with whipped farm-fresh organic cream (SEE RECIPE, PAGE 173) is also delicious.

Decorate the table with something that comes from nature. I like to use grapes and vines from our grape arbor. The gorgeous green leaves that have begun to change colors are beautiful accents for a fall table. In these pictures I use old silver plates and sugar bowls to act as separate centerpieces on the table. I chose olive green, brown, and Tuscan gold as my color palette. I used vintage Rosanna "French Toile" dinner plates and Rosanna tortoise-colored flatware. Handmade place cards fashioned from heavy Italian watercolor paper add warmth and texture to the table arrangement.

Invite someone to share in your Thanksgiving who is alone and far from family. It is the spirit of Thanksgiving to invite those far from loved ones to partake in the lovely tradition of sharing nature's bounty among friends.

fall recipes

Rosanna's Thanksgiving Turkey

Rubbing the meat under the skin of the turkey with a flavorful paste of herbs, garlic, and prosciutto and letting it marinate in the refrigerator overnight ensures that it stays juicy as it roasts. Garnish the platter of sliced turkey with big branches of fresh rosemary and sage.

The size of the turkey will determine the number of servings. I would figure on 1 pound (454 g) of uncooked turkey per person.

Cooking Chart

8 to 12 pounds (3 to 5 kg) (2 to 4 people): 2¾–3 hours

12 to 16 pounds (5 to 7 kg) (5 to 7 people): 3½–4 hours

16 to 20 pounds (7 to 9 kg) (8 to 10 people): 4¼–4¾ hours

20 to 24 pounds (9 to 11 kg) (11 to 13 people): 4½–5 hours

3 large sprigs fresh rosemary, stemmed

15 large leaves fresh sage

8 cloves garlic

1 tablespoon (12 g) plus 1 teaspoon (6 g) coarse sea salt

4 slices prosciutto

½ cup (125 ml) extra-virgin olive oil, plus more for drizzling

1 organic, hormone-free turkey, preferably free-range, cleaned, giblets removed

1 large carrot

½ onion

1 rib celery

Fine sea salt

Put the rosemary, sage, 5 cloves of the garlic, 1 tablespoon (12 g) of the coarse salt, and the prosciutto on a board and mince them together. Drizzle the oil over the mixture and mince until the mixture is a thick paste.

Place the turkey in a large stainless-steel, porcelain, or ovenproof glass roasting pan. Gently pull up the skin near the cavity and rub small spoonfuls of the herb mixture under the skin, pushing it all the way to the back of the breast. Make sure the breast is totally covered with the herb mixture. Put a heaping tablespoon of the mixture in the cavity of the turkey and rub it all over the inside. Put the carrot, onion, celery, and remaining 3 cloves of garlic in the cavity and sprinkle the 1 teaspoon (6 g) of coarse salt inside the cavity. (The carrot and celery should be whole when inserted in the cavity with the half onion.)

Rub the remaining mixture all over the top (breast) and bottom (back) of the turkey, as well as the legs. Generously season with fine salt all over the turkey and drizzle with more oil. Let the turkey marinate overnight.

The next day (Thanksgiving), preheat the oven to 475°F (246°C) (Gas mark 9).

Roast for 20 to 25 minutes to brown the turkey. Lower the oven temperature to 325°F (163°C) (Gas mark 3) and roast until the meat between the breast and leg registers 170°F (77°C) and the thigh 180°F (82°C) on an instant-read meat thermometer (see cooking chart, left), basting the turkey often with the pan juices to ensure a juicy turkey. The turkey is done when the drumstick moves easily and the juices run clear, not pink. Let the turkey rest, loosely covered with aluminum foil that does not touch the turkey, for at least 30 minutes before carving.

Make the gravy (following page), if desired, then slice the turkey and serve.

Gravy

If your turkey-roasting pan is not flameproof, transfer the drippings to a saucepan to make the gravy.

SERVES 8

1 tablespoon (14 g) unsalted butter

2 tablespoons all-purpose flour

Drippings from Rosanna's Thanksgiving Turkey (PAGE 126), clear fat skimmed off

½ cup (125 ml) dry white wine

Sea salt

In a small saucepan over medium heat, melt the butter, then whisk in the flour. Cook the roux, whisking frequently, until the butter is a shade darker, but not browned, about 1 minute. Whisk the roux into the drippings in the roasting pan or another saucepan set over medium heat and cook, whisking constantly, until the roux is incorporated into the drippings. Add the wine and cook until the liquid is reduced by three-quarters. Taste and add more salt if necessary. Serve in a sauceboat and drizzle the sliced turkey with the gravy before serving.

Oven-Roasted Halloween Pumpkin Seeds

These are great snacks for children, and, for adults, wonderful with a glass of robust red wine!

Raw pumpkin seeds, from a jack-o'-lantern

Extra-virgin olive oil

Fine sea salt

Preheat the oven to 250°F (121°C) (Gas mark 1).

Put the pumpkin seeds in a colander and rinse and use your hands to remove all the orange pulp from the seeds. The seeds will be very slippery.

Lightly coat a baking sheet with oil. Spread the pumpkin seeds out on the baking sheet and toss to coat them with oil. The seeds should not be floating in oil, just covered lightly.

Season the seeds generously with salt.

Bake for 2 to 3 hours, until golden brown, turning them occasionally so that they brown evenly. The seeds should roast very slowly. Remove from the oven and taste for salt. If needed, add another sprinkling of sea salt. Let cool completely, then store in an airtight container.

Thanksgiving Squash

One of my favorite dishes from childhood was my mother's roasted acorn squash. The preparation was simple, but the favors were complex and delicious. The squash's bare hint of sweetness and spice makes it a sophisticated but crowd-pleasing substitute for the traditional yams.

SERVES 8

4 acorn squashes, halved, seeds removed

8 teaspoons (37 g) unsalted butter

8 tablespoons (86 g) brown sugar

Ground cinnamon

Preheat the oven to 350°F (177°C) (Gas mark 4).

Arrange the squash halves cut side up on baking sheets. In each squash half place 1 teaspoon of the butter, 1 tablespoon (10 g) of the brown sugar, and a dash of cinnamon. Bake for about 1 hour, until the flesh of the squash is soft when pierced with a fork and the sides look slightly caved in. Let the squash rest for 15 minutes before serving.

Roasted Potato Wedges with Olive Oil and Oregano

SERVES 8

6 russet potatoes

¼ cup (60 ml) extra-virgin olive oil

1 teaspoon (5 g) dried Italian oregano

1 teaspoon (6 g) sea salt

Preheat the oven to 350°F (177°C) (Gas mark 4).

Cut the potatoes into eight wedges each, leaving the skin on. Pour the oil in the bottom of a baking dish. Put the potatoes in the pan and toss to coat with the oil. Rub the oregano between the palms of your hands to release the flavor and sprinkle it over the potatoes. Sprinkle the salt over the potatoes.

Bake for 45 minutes to 1 hour, until golden brown, turning the potatoes often so they brown evenly and become crunchy. Serve hot.

Thanksgiving Roasted Vegetables

These are delicious caramelized vegetables that melt in your mouth. And even if you have never liked Brussels sprouts before, after tasting these they could well become your new favorite vegetable.

SERVES 6

¼ cup (60 ml) plus two tablespoons (20g) extra-virgin olive oil

1 sprig fresh rosemary, stemmed

2 cloves garlic, minced

1 teaspoon (6 g) sea salt

1 pound (474 g) Brussels sprouts, trimmed

8 carrots, cut into 1½-inch (4 cm) lengths

3 red bell peppers, quartered, seeds and membranes removed

3 green bell peppers, quartered, seeds and membranes removed

6 small yellow onions, peeled and cut into quarters

Preheat the oven to 325°F (163°C) (Gas mark 3).

In a large roasting pan, combine the oil, rosemary, garlic, and salt. Put the remaining ingredients in the pan and toss to coat the vegetables with the oil. Bake for about 1 hour, stirring every 15 minutes, until soft and caramelized.

Arrange on a large oval tray and serve.

Rosanna's Lentil Soup

Like the chicken soup on page 168, this soup makes an excellent lunch to take to school or work the next day, so be sure to save some for the Thermos.

SERVES 8

1 pound small green lentils

½ cup (120 ml) extra-virgin olive oil

3 ribs celery, diced

2 carrots, diced

1 sweet onion, diced

5 cloves garlic, minced

2 quarts (2 liters) organic chicken broth

Soak the lentils in a bowl of water for 1 hour. Drain and set aside.

Put the oil in a large saucepan and place over medium heat. When the oil is hot, add the vegetables and sauté until they are just soft, about 5 minutes. Add the lentils and sauté for 5 minutes.

Add the broth. Bring to a simmer and cook, covered, over low heat for about 1½ hours, until the lentils are soft. Serve with crusty bread drizzled with extra-virgin olive oil.

Timballo di Spinaci (Spinach Soufflé)

This is an Italian version of the French soufflé, but much easier to make. Mix up a few ingredients, put it in the oven, and voilà!

SERVES 6

2 (10-ounce) (284 g) boxes chopped frozen spinach, thawed. Take the spinach out of the package and put it in a colander set over a plate. Thaw overnight in the refrigerator.

5 eggs, lightly beaten

1½ cups ricotta

6 tablespoons (60 g) all-purpose flour

½ cube (7 g) salted butter, melted

1 cup (100 g) freshly grated Parmigiano-Reggiano cheese

½ teaspoon (3 g) sea salt

Preheat the oven to 350°F (177°C) (Gas mark 4). Butter a 2-quart (2-liter) lidded casserole dish.

Squeeze the spinach in the colander until all the water is removed. Put the spinach in a bowl. Add the eggs and ricotta and stir to combine. Stir in the flour and butter, then the Parmigiano-Reggiano and salt.

Transfer the mixture to the prepared dish, cover, and bake for 1 hour, or until golden brown. Serve hot.

My Mother's Apple Dumplings

These dumplings are wonderful dolloped with something creamy—good-quality vanilla ice cream, whipped cream, or Greek yogurt sweetened to taste with a bit of honey.

SERVES 8

For the apples:

2 cups (344 g) packed brown sugar

1 cup (2 sticks) (226 g) unsalted butter, softened

1 teaspoon (5 g) ground cinnamon

1 teaspoon (5 g) freshly grated nutmeg

8 Gala apples, peeled and cored

For the dough:

4 cups (568 g) all-purpose flour

1 teaspoon (6 g) salt

1½ cups (3 sticks) (339 g) unsalted butter, cut into 1-inch (2.5 cm) cubes

2 tablespoons (20 g) vegetable shortening

½ cup (125 ml) ice water

To bake:

8 pats unsalted butter

Cinnamon sugar

Make the apples: In a small bowl, combine the brown sugar, butter, cinnamon, and nutmeg. Fill the centers of the apples with the mixture. Set aside.

Make the dough: Put the flour and salt in a food processor and pulse to combine. Add the cubed butter and shortening and pulse until just incorporated. Slowly add the ice water through the feed tube and pulse until a ball forms. Do not overwork the dough. Flatten two disks of dough and wrap in plastic for about 1 hour.

Preheat the oven to 375°F (191°C) (Gas mark 5).

On a pastry cloth, using a floured rolling pin covered with a pastry stocking, roll out the dough into a rough square ⅛ inch (3 mm) thick. Cut into 8 squares and set a filled apple in the center of each square. Bring the corners of the dough up to cover the entire apple and pinch the top to seal. Repeat with the remaining apples and dough. Place the dumplings on a rimmed baking sheet.

Bake the dumplings: Dot the tops of the dumplings with butter and sprinkle with cinnamon sugar to taste. Bake for 40 to 60 minutes, until the apple is tender when pierced carefully with a fork. Let cool a bit, then serve warm or at room temperature in individual serving bowls.

After-School Wild Blackberry Pie

My mother grew up a simple farm girl from Kansas. She learned the best of the region's cooking, and that meant out-of-this-world delicious homemade fruit and cream pies.

MAKES 1 (9-INCH) (23 CM) PIE; SERVES 6 TO 8

1 tablespoon (10 g) all-purpose flour

1 tablespoon melted butter plus ¼ cup (½ stick) (57 g) cold unsalted butter, cut into cubes

2 pints (4 cups) (448 g) fresh wild blackberries

1 cup sugar (200 g) or honey (340 g), plus 1 teaspoon (5 g) sugar for sprinkling

My Mom's Extra-Flaky Pie Crust Dough (RECIPE ON PAGE 138)

Preheat the oven to 350°F (177°C) (Gas mark 4).

In a small pan, stir together the flour and 1 tablespoon (14 g) melted butter. Heat briefly on the stove. Set aside.

In a colander, rinse the blackberries gently under cold running water. Drain thoroughly, then put the blackberries in a bowl and add the 1 cup sugar, the cubed butter, and the melted butter and flour mixture. Stir gently, using a folding motion, until just combined, being careful not to crush the blackberries. Set aside.

On a pastry cloth, using a floured rolling pin covered with a pastry stocking, roll one ball of the dough out into a 12 ½-inch (31 cm) circle. Slip a pie pan under the dough and gently adjust it to fit the pan. Fill with the blackberry mixture.

Roll the second ball of dough out into a circle and cut it into 2-inch-wide (5 cm) strips. Place the strips of dough over the filling, first horizontally, then vertically, to form a checkerboard of crust. Pinch the edges to attach them to the bottom crust, then use your knuckle to form a fluted edge around the pie. Sprinkle the top dough with the 1 teaspoon of sugar.

Bake for about 1 hour, or until the filling is bubbling and has thickened and the top crust is golden brown. Let cool for at least 1 hour, then slice and serve.

Golden Harvest Peach Pie

This came from my mother's repertoire of recipes. At harvest time, she would go to the farms around Portland, Oregon, and hand pick her own peaches. Thus, this delicious peach pie was lovingly created.

MAKES 1 (9-INCH) (23 CM) PIE; SERVES 6 TO 8

2 tablespoons (20 g) all-purpose flour

2 tablespoons melted butter plus ½ cup (1 stick) (113 g) unsalted butter, cut into cubes

7 large ripe peaches

1 cup sugar (200 g) or honey (340 g), plus 1 teaspoon (5 g) sugar for sprinkling

½ teaspoon (2.5 g) ground cinnamon

My Mom's Extra-Flaky Pie Crust Dough (RECIPE ON PAGE 138)

Preheat the oven to 350°F (177°C) (Gas mark 4).

In a small pan, stir together the flour and 2 tablespoons melted butter. Heat briefly on the stove. Set aside.

Fill a large pot with water and bring to a boil. Add 3 or 4 peaches and blanch until the skin appears slightly blistered, 1 to 2 minutes. Using a slotted spoon, gently remove the peaches to a colander. Blanch the remaining peaches and add them to the colander. Let the peaches cool for 10 minutes, then use a dull knife to gently peel them. Slice the peaches ½ inch thick, then put them in a bowl and add the 1 cup of sugar, the cubed butter, the flour mixture, and the cinnamon. Stir gently, using a folding motion, until just combined, being careful not to bruise the peaches. Set aside.

On a pastry cloth, using a floured rolling pin covered with a pastry stocking, roll one ball of the dough out into a 12 ½-inch (31 cm) circle. Slip a pie pan under the dough and gently adjust it to fit the pan. Fill with the peach mixture.

Roll the second ball of dough out into a circle and cut it into 2-inch-wide (5 cm) strips. Place the strips of dough over the filling, first horizontally, then vertically, to form a checkerboard of crust. Pinch the edges to attach them to the bottom crust, then use your knuckle to form a fluted edge around the pie. Sprinkle the top dough with the 1 teaspoon of sugar.

Bake for about 1 hour, or until the filling is bubbling and has become firm and the top crust is golden brown. Let cool for at least 1 hour, then slice and serve.

Cinnamon Crust

This was my favorite treat as a child. When my mother made pies, she'd let me use the scraps of dough to make a delicious cinnamon-sugar pastry. My children and husband love this part of the pie. They gobble it down within minutes after it has cooled.

Pie dough scraps

Butter

Sugar

Ground cinnamon

Roll out the dough, in whatever shape; it can be misshapen. Place the dough in a small pie plate. Put small pats of butter all over the dough, then sprinkle with sugar and cinnamon. Fold the edges up to make an envelope. Dot with more butter and dust the top with cinnamon and sugar.

Bake at 350°F (177°C) (Gas mark 4) for about 15 minutes, until the crust is golden brown and the sugar is bubbling. Let cool, cut into small wedges, and enjoy!

My Mom's Extra-Flaky Pie Crust Dough

Make sure that you don't work the dough too much or the crust will be tough and not flaky.

MAKES ENOUGH FOR 1 (9-INCH) (23 CM) DOUBLE-CRUST PIE, OR 2 (9-INCH) (23 CM) SINGLE-CRUST PIES

4 cups (512 g) all-purpose flour

1 teaspoon (6 g) finely ground sea salt

1½ cup (3 sticks) (340 g) cold organic unsalted butter, cut into cubes

⅛ cup (28 g) cold organic vegetable shortening

½ cup (125 ml) ice water

Put the flour and salt in a food processor and pulse to combine. Add the butter in small pieces and shortening and pulse until the mixture resembles fine cornmeal.

While pulsing the motor, slowly add the ½ cup (125 ml) ice water through the feed tube. If the dough has not formed a ball, add a little more water, pulsing until the dough forms a firm ball. Do not overprocess or the dough will be tough. Divide the dough in half and wrap each ball in plastic wrap. Set aside in the refrigerator for 1 hour before proceeding with the pie or tart recipe.

Grandma's Caramel Cake

This recipe comes from my grandmother Ruth Edwards, who was born in the heartland of America. Her homemade cakes were legendary.

MAKES 1 (8-INCH) (20 CM) CAKE; SERVES 6 TO 8

For the yellow cake layers

2⅔ cups (292 g) cake flour, plus more for pans

2¼ teaspoons (14 g) baking powder

½ teaspoon (3 g) salt

1 cup (2 sticks) (226 g) unsalted butter

2 cups (400 g) sifted sugar

4 large eggs, separated

1½ teaspoons (23 ml) vanilla extract

1 cup (250 ml) milk

For the brown-sugar frosting

1½ cups (258 g) packed brown sugar

½ cup (118 ml) heavy cream, plus more if necessary

2 tablespoons (28 g) unsalted butter

⅛ teaspoon (.7 g) salt

½ teaspoon (2.5 ml) vanilla extract

1 cup (113 g) confectioners' sugar

Make the cake layers: Preheat the oven to 350°F (177°C) (Gas mark 4). Butter 2 (8-inch) (20 cm) round cake pans and dust them with flour.

Sift the flour, baking powder, and salt together into a medium bowl. Set aside.

In a large bowl, using an electric mixer, beat the butter until soft. Continuing to beat, add the sugar slowly, then beat until the mixture is very light and fluffy. Beat in the egg yolks, one at a time, beating well after each addition, then stir in the vanilla. Add the flour mixture and stir to combine, then stir in the milk.

In a separate bowl, using a whisk or clean beaters, beat the egg whites until stiff peaks form. Gently fold them into the batter. Divide between the prepared pans and bake for 30 to 35 minutes, until a toothpick inserted in the center comes out clean. Let cool in the pans on wire racks for 5 minutes, then invert the pans and remove the cakes. Let cool completely.

Make the brown-sugar frosting: Combine the brown sugar, ½ cup (125 ml) cream, the butter, and the salt in a large saucepan and cook over medium heat, stirring frequently, until the mixture just comes to a boil. Remove from the heat, transfer to a mixing bowl, and add the vanilla and confectioners' sugar. Using an electric mixer, beat on high speed until smooth and creamy. If the frosting is too dry, add a bit more cream. It should be thick and easy to spread.

Assemble the cake: Put one cake layer on a cake stand and frost the top. Add the second layer and frost the top and sides. Serve.

Owl Cookies

My mother made these owl cookies every Halloween. Charming and delicious, they were always a hit with my friends. The dough is a basic refrigerator-cookie dough that is made ahead of time and can be also frozen. Children love to assemble and decorate these cookies, which feature chocolate chips for eyes and a giant salted cashew for a nose to make up the perfect owl face.

This recipe makes a good-sized batch of large cookies for Halloween school parties or Halloween parties at home.

MAKES ABOUT 18 COOKIES

3 cups (426 g) all-purpose flour

3 teaspoons (18 g) baking powder

½ teaspoon (3 g) sea salt

1¼ cups (2½ sticks) (286 g) unsalted butter at room temperature

1⅓ cups (267 g) sugar

2 large eggs

4 teaspoons (20 ml) vanilla extract

½ (12-ounce) (340 g) bag semisweet chocolate chips, melted

For decorating and baking

Semisweet chocolate chips

About 18 whole roasted and salted cashews (or candy corn, if nut allergies are a concern)

In a large bowl, combine the flour, baking powder, and salt.

In a large bowl, using an electric mixer, beat the butter until soft. Continuing to beat, add the sugar slowly, then beat until the mixture is very light and fluffy. Mix in the dry ingredients.

In a small bowl, beat together the eggs and vanilla, then add them to the dough a little at a time, mixing well after each addition.

Transfer about one-third of the dough to a separate bowl and stir in the melted chocolate chips to make a chocolate dough. Shape the chocolate dough into a 10-inch-long (25 cm) log, working very quickly before the chocolate solidifies. Wrap in wax paper and put in the refrigerator.

Roll out the remaining dough (vanilla) into a long rectangular shape as long as the chocolate log. Set the chilled chocolate log in the center of the vanilla rectangle and wrap it up so that a cross-section resembles a bulls-eye, with a vanilla outer layer and a chocolate center. Wrap the log in wax paper and refrigerate until firm, at least 2 hours; you can freeze the dough for up to 1 month.

Decorate and bake the cookies: Preheat the oven to 375°F (191°C) (Gas mark 4). Butter 2 baking sheets. Place the chocolate chips and cashews in small bowls for easy access.

Unwrap the logs and cut them into ⅛-inch (3 mm) slices. Join the two slices together by placing them side by side on a baking sheet and pinching them. Slightly pinch the two opposite sides of the rounds into pointy ear shapes. Place a chocolate chip upside down in the center of each chocolate eye, then embed a cashew into the center of the two joined circles. Repeat with the remaining slices, spacing the owls 2 inches (5 cm) apart on the baking sheets. Bake for about 10 minutes, watching closely, until lightly browned. Transfer the cookies to a wire rack to cool completely.

Store the cookies in a large tin, with the layers separated by sheets of wax paper. Keep the tin in a cool place until Halloween, or freeze the cookies ahead of time. Be careful not to fill the tin too full to avoid breaking the two halves apart. Serve on a shiny black cake pedestal for a very spooky effect.

Pumpkin and Cat Cupcakes

I am a busy working mother, and I don't always have time to make my own cupcakes from scratch. Dr. Oetker's organic cake mixes (from Germany) are not only quick and easy to use, but tasty and healthful as well, especially if you use organic eggs and milk. You can find Dr. Oetker's online or at your local organic food store. I use both the vanilla and chocolate mixes.

MAKES 24 CUPCAKES

Cupcakes made from 1 box each Dr. Oetker Organics vanilla and chocolate cake mixes, cooled completely

1 recipe Rosanna's Quick Cupcake Frosting

Orange fruit leather

Grape fruit leather

Panda soft licorice whips

White chocolate chips

For pumpkin faces: Frost the cupcakes with plain white frosting. Cut the orange fruit leather into triangles for eyes and half-moon shapes for mouths. Cut a small square out of the mouth piece for the tooth of the pumpkin.

For cat faces: Frost the cupcakes. Cut each licorice whip into 3 lengths; they will serve as the eyes (SEE THE PHOTO). For the nose, place a white chocolate chip upside down. Cut more licorice whips into 2-inch skinny strips and place 2 on each side of the nose for whiskers and 1 underneath for a sad mouth.

Rosanna's Quick Cupcake Frosting

MAKES 2 CUPS; ENOUGH TO FROST 22 TO 24 CUPCAKES.

4 tablespoons (60 g) unsalted butter

2 cups (226 g) confectioners' sugar

3 tablespoons (40 ml) heavy cream

4 tablespoons (60 ml) whole milk, or more if necessary

½ teaspoon (2.5 ml) vanilla extract

Dash of salt

1 or 2 drops food coloring or 1 cup (182.4 g) semi-sweet chocolate chips, melted (optional)

In a large bowl, using an electric mixer, beat the butter until soft and creamy. Add the confectioners' sugar and mix well, then add the cream and beat until smooth. Slowly add the milk, vanilla, and salt, mixing to combine; if the frosting is too thick to spread, add more milk. To make chocolate frosting, add one cup of melted semi-sweet chocolate chips to the vanilla frosting

winter

Winter is a

challenging season

The weather turns cold, inhibiting our ability to connect with others, at times making us feel isolated and alone. This loneliness is particularly true for those in need, those who lack the basic comforts that help to fend off the creeping chill of winter isolation.

Winter is a time when we must make an extra effort to interact with our friends, family, and neighbors. This is why holidays, celebrations, and lighthearted moments of frivolity take center stage this time of year. Coming together helps us make it through the dark months. The cold season is also, of course, a time when giving of yourself—donating to charities, volunteering your time and skills to help others, and doing good deeds in general—is perhaps most important and appreciated.

Establish Traditions and Rituals

Practicing rituals and traditions is vital to creating and sustaining a well-lived life. The repetition of traditions and rituals helps us grow roots; it allows us to take part in a legacy spanning many generations. When we practice a tradition, we are in fact linking ourselves to the chain of human history, providing a continuation of the kind of life that humans have lived since the beginning of civilization.

Celebrate the winter months by making them festive. Plan occasions — dinner dates, holiday parties, theater outings, and cocktail rendezvous — to gather your loved ones, friends and family alike.

Each individual has his or her own traditions and rituals that signify something special and unique. The winter months give us many opportunities to establish traditions that can last for generations. One of my own traditions is to prepare a special Italian dinner every Christmas Eve: risotto with osso bucco (ITALIAN RICE WITH VEAL SHANKS; SEE RECIPES, PAGES 169 AND 171). My family looks forward to the evening not just because it's a holiday, but because they know we'll be eating one of their favorite meals that comes around only once a year.

Another unique tradition: When my family decorates the Christmas tree, I make hot toddies and my mother's Christmas sugar cookies (SEE RECIPES, PAGES 177 AND 174) and serve them in Rosanna Christmas mugs and dessert plates. I use the same mugs every year to start off the holiday season. I play a variety of Christmas music, including jazz renditions sung by Frank Sinatra and Ella Fitzgerald, and classical pieces by Luciano Pavarotti and Placido Domingo. For my family, this night represents the beginning of winter holiday festivities. Together we transform the house, and when we're finished, we find ourselves surrounded by the magical beauty of the holidays.

Cooking special food is an important aspect of creating a holiday atmosphere. Making a dish that may be a bit more elaborate than usual not only makes the meal feel festive, but also can bring people together in the kitchen as everyone pitches in to help. Each Christmas, I make two savory Italian dishes to eat as an appetizer for brunch on Christmas morning. One dish, called *erbazzone*, comes from Reggio Emilia, the Italian town where my grandmother was born. It's a decadent spinach, cheese, and egg mixture enfolded in flaky pastry (SEE RECIPE, PAGE 164). The richness of the filling, and the care that I take with the pastry, help to mark the meal as a grand occasion. My family loves my *erbazzone* so much that it's practically gone as soon as I set it down on the table—and that's reason enough to make it.

The second recipe comes from Perugia, the Italian university town where I studied abroad during my junior year of college. *Torta rustica* is a savory tart made from three cheeses and prosciutto ham covered with a melt-in-your-mouth pastry crust (SEE RECIPE, PAGE 166). Like *erbazzone, torta rustica* disappears within seconds.

When I set my table, I always use the same Rosanna holiday dishes that I've used for years. Sometimes I also mix in my mother's vintage silver and porcelain serving pieces, which in turn came from my grandmother's china cabinet. I incorporate these family heirlooms to create a table that shows the layers of our family's history.

Opening one Christmas gift on Christmas Eve is another special tradition my daughters, Alessandra and Francesca, always look forward to. With the family gathered by the tree, the room lit by tiny lights and candles, and perhaps a warming fire, we sip hot drinks and keep the cold and dark at bay for a while.

These are only a few of the rituals my family practices during the holidays. Of course, there are as many ways to celebrate the holidays of the season as there are nationalities and religions and cultures. With such a variety of ceremonies and rites that have been passed down through the ages, you can simply choose to continue with established cultural traditions or create brand-new traditions with special significances that are distinctly yours. Tradition is the glue that binds us together and makes the holidays a time that everyone looks forward to celebrating.

Make Memories

All it takes to make a memory is generosity of spirit. A lasting memory could be something as simple as a yearly photo with Santa. Once you establish a tradition, the memories create themselves. Making a memory is a wonderful and selfless gift. With time and effort, you can give a gift that is far more profound than a material object. Nothing serves us better than a store of good memories during more difficult times.

It's said that young children remember events from their very early childhoods much more clearly if those activities are repeated throughout the years—and the same may be true of adults. An event that lodges in the mind, if repeated as a tradition or ritual, can bring back pleasant memories that might otherwise have been lost to time and age. Make an effort to create special occasions, and set them in your loved ones' memories by establishing them as a tradition, however loose and informal, and your gift of those memories is likely to be enjoyed for years to come.

Embrace Nostalgia—on Your Own Terms

The holidays can be a very emotional time. Memories of past holidays creep into our consciousnesses, creating an atmosphere that is both beautiful and bittersweet. Embrace the happy memories of the winter holidays from the past, celebrating your own personal history in a way that makes you and those close to you happy. If you don't have many good holiday memories, create some! With the new year close at hand, you should feel especially free to shake off the remnants of a less-than-ideal past with new friends and new traditions.

And remember that nothing can make you feel better than giving. The winter holidays are the ideal time to go beyond yourself and give to others. The winter months provide endless opportunities to embrace beauty and good, and volunteering—working hard and thinking of people other than yourself—can be an amazing distraction when the holiday (or post-holiday) doldrums hit.

Cocoon

Wintertime presents us with challenges both physical and psychological: It's important to keep the body warm and the spirit uplifted. Make an effort to keep out the cold that can enter the body and spirit during the winter months.

When the days are cold, the sky is gray, and dark evenings approach right on the heels of the workday, taking on any tasks other than those necessary for survival can be daunting. As the weather outside turns dark and foreboding, for example, I dread leaving my office to travel home in the dark. To ward off the surrounding blackness, I immediately turn on the radio in my car and listen to something that makes me feel good—fabulous jazz, oldies, or classical music. Doing this lifts my mood considerably. When I arrive home, I light candles and turn on small table lamps to create a halo of warmth and security. I make myself a cup of English Breakfast Tea (no matter that it's nighttime: I like this strong black tea at any hour). I change into warm and comfortable clothes, like my favorite soft cashmere socks, which instantly warm my feet. Now, I'm ready to shift gears and go into cocooning mode. I begin by cooking dinner for my family. One of my favorite meals

to serve during the cold months is a chicken soup made from the remains of the previous night's roast (SEE RECIPES, PAGES 167 AND 168). Because the chicken carcass is already well seasoned, I don't need to add anything besides vegetables—carrots, celery, and small red potatoes—sea salt, large egg noodles such as pappardelle, and water. It's easy, and doesn't require much thought after a draining day. I serve the soup with crusty bread and a rich red wine. My family loves this meal. In one bowl we find the perfect combination of ingredients for warming our bodies and restoring our spirits after a long day of school and work. I always make extra to warm up in the morning and pack for my daughter's school lunch. Francesca has a warm meal with great nutritional value that also says, "I love you," because I prepared it myself.

There are so many ways we can create a feeling of warmth, small ways of cocooning in our everyday lives. One of the simplest ways to do this in the winter—even when you're out and about, and curling up with a novel on the couch is not feasible—is to dress in layers. Select warm, natural fabrics that protect you from the elements and feel good against your body: soft 100 percent cotton is particularly luscious followed by fine merino wool or cashmere, or even flannel. One item I practically never remove during the winter is a basic soft cotton knit tank. Make sure it's made of a combed fabric, because this piece of clothing lies closest to your body. It is perhaps the most essential article in keeping your body warm. There are many stores that carry wonderful, high-quality tanks, soft and durable, that fit a woman's body, and many retailers offer them in dozens of cheerful colors. A soft and snuggly merino or cashmere sweater over a tank is one of the wisest investments you can make when it comes to keeping the cold out.

Another easy way to keep the body warm is to drink hot beverages throughout the day. Sipping a great cup of coffee, a fine tea, or a treat like dark and creamy hot cocoa—and taking a moment to truly appreciate it—can give the body an instant and much-needed lift on a bone-chilling day. Another trick I learned from my mother is to drink a mug of warm water. As she always told me, "Drinking hot water is like taking a bath inside your body." The water cleanses your system, moving out toxins and providing a sense of refreshment without caffeine or sugar.

While you're cocooning and staying warm and snug indoors, don't forget to venture out into the sunlight as often as possible. Even if the temperatures are forbidding, light itself—and preferably natural light— is essential to keeping our moods bright.

Create an Atmosphere

Since humans first raised their voices in song, music has offered a way to soothe a ruffled soul. When you have the opportunity, play music to improve your mood, whether you need invigoration or calming down. For creating a cheery, laid-back vibe, I'm particularly fond of Brazilian jazz artists like Antonio Carlos Jobim, Joaõ Gilberto, Stan Getz (during his bossa nova years), Bebel Gilberto, and Astrud Gilberto. American jazz musicians and singers like Chet Baker, Ella Fitzgerald, Erroll Garner, Frank Sinatra, Sarah Vaughan, Oscar Peterson, and Billie Holiday can bring a calm sophistication to the table. Opera, like Puccini's *La Bohème* or recordings by Placido Domingo, can either slip into the background in a soothing way or encourage you to fully focus as a listener. French modernist composer Erik Satie's *Gnossienne No. 1* and *Les Trois Gymnopédies* are breathtaking pieces that inspire thoughtful meditation and reflection. For everyday listening pleasure, I enjoy the soundtracks from movies like *Pride and Prejudice*, *The Painted Veil*, *Cinema Paradiso*, *The English Patient*, *Out of Africa*, and Claude Lelouche's *A Man and a Woman*, which never fail to send me to a heavenly, otherworldly place.

To complement the aural atmosphere, drape a string of white lights across a mantel or bunch them in beautiful red hurricane vases. Light creates magical moments, and the winter months certainly do need lights to brighten the darkness. You'll find that against this rich aesthetic backdrop, you've created a space for personal growth and valuable introspection. Playing music during your main meal of the day, and lighting candles or tiny strand lights, can transform an ordinary setting—your kitchen or your dining room—into someplace magical. These are inexpensive and simple ways to lift the mood and transport your spirit to another level.

Taking warm baths not only lends a sense of ritual to an everyday task but also provides a wonderful way to keep a healthy balance between the hectic outside world and your calm inner life. Put on some music, place lit candles around the tub, use a lovely scented soap to soothe your body, and apply moisturizing lotion afterward. It is a simple act, yet wholly restorative.

Give of Yourself

There is no better season than frigid, gray winter for giving, for going outside your own comfort zone and reaching out to others. This is the time to stop and take inventory of the positive aspects of your life and to share your good fortune with others, to connect with family and friends, and to build community. Each winter, resurrect established traditions that demonstrate a commitment to giving. There is a long history of making financial contributions to charitable organizations or to individuals who are less fortunate than ourselves, but there's no reason to stop there. Donating your time and efforts on behalf of others is the ultimate gift, whether it means baking holiday treats for family and friends, volunteering for the cause of your choice, or reaching out beyond yourself in some other way.

It is in the act of giving that we realize our true potential to create a better world.

To be clear, giving means not only the giving of material goods, money, or time, but also the giving of personal energy. It's giving of the self that warms the heart of those around us. Strike up a conversation with a stranger in the grocery store or on the subway. Smile as you let another driver merge ahead of you onto the highway. Look your friend in the eyes when you're listening to her tell you about a hard day at work. The world can be a lonely and isolated place, especially during the winter, and something as simple as a meaningful exchange of eye contact or an unexpected conversation can make all the difference in the quality of your day and those of the people around you.

Doing a simple good deed that doesn't involve spending money is deeply appreciated—it's the kind of gesture that's too often missing in today's society. One of my neighbors, with whom we share a driveway, treks up our steep lane to pick up the daily newspaper. My neighbor rises earlier than I do in the mornings, and out of pure generosity gathers my paper as well as her own and has delivered it to my door before I've even had my first cup of coffee. This favor warms my heart. Her thoughtfulness helps me begin my day with a smile on my face and renewed hope that our society isn't yet fragmented beyond repair. Gestures like these, of genuine kindness, make my life richer and make me feel more connected to my community as a whole, and I try to return them in kind whenever I can.

The Magic of Homemaking

Sadly, we're living in an era when barely anyone has the time to enjoy the luxury—yes, the luxury—of home-making. Many people buy prepared meals, don't bother to set the table, and can't find the time to fit in a meal at which the whole family dines together. They look on cleaning, doing laundry, and cooking as obligations to be dreaded. Many people think of household chores as drudgery, but I don't agree in the slightest. I think of these basic elements of creating a home as the glue that keeps us together; they're vital to feeling that you're a part of a

family and community. Homemaking can be a profound act, one that connects a family and enriches the lives of those who receive this special kind of care. Consider homemaking to be a way of nourishing a family's soul rather than an obnoxious obligation, and what was once drudgery is transformed into an act of love.

When I set my table, I imagine my family sitting around it. I prepare meals that nourish not only their bodies but also their souls, and I think of my family and guests as I work: How will Francesca like the pasta? Perhaps I'll add a bit more chile to the sauce, because she mentioned enjoying the spiciness the last time we had *puttanesca* for dinner. When I wash the dishes, I feel an intimate connection to my family because we've just shared a wonderful meal together, and it was all centered around these plates and forks and spoons. When

I lovingly put them away in the cupboard I think of the next meal we'll sit down to together. Amid a full and hectic life, seemingly unnecessary chores—setting the table with care, gently hand washing dishes and glassware (even ones that would probably be just fine in the dishwasher), sweeping up the kitchen afterward with a good straw broom—can be relaxing and mind-clearing, requiring as they do a certain methodical slowness, a carefulness that precludes haste or overthinking.

The various tasks that make up homemaking are rituals that remind me how blessed I am to have a family. All it takes to improve your outlook on household chores is a change in the way you view homemaking: Seeing it not as an annoyance but as a natural expression of love will make taking care of your loved ones a joy.

The holidays provide a catalyst for recalling the good times. Share these positive memories with the friends and loved ones who helped create them, and use the holidays to encourage more memory making.

Make Time for Introspection

During the winter months, we have the opportunity to reconnect with our inner lives. The inclement weather allows us to concentrate on the richness that comes out of quietude and slowness, and we light candles to illuminate the long, dark hours.

I love a good movie, and during the holidays I delve into a host of old favorites—*It's a Wonderful Life, White Christmas, The Bishop's Wife, Love Actually,* and, for a bit of silly fun, *Elf.* In their own ways, each of these films strikes a chord within me. During winter, I pull out several films that help make me forget the cold, depressing weather by transporting me to another time and place. *Pride & Prejudice* with Keira Knightley, Gwynneth Paltrow's *Emma,* the Ang Lee–directed *Sense and Sensibility,* and *Enchanted April* are a few films I cannot live without. Others that touch me include *Shakespeare in Love, Little Women, Chocolat, A Room with a View,* and *The Painted Veil.* For comedy, I unfailingly turn to Woody's Allen's *Annie Hall* and Rob Reiner's *When Harry Met Sally.*

These films are my secret to escape. Each one models the triumph of the human spirit, and during times of physical and psychological transition they become sources of great affirmation and hope.

Enjoy the Festivities

Since ancient times, humans have filled the winter months with festivities that are based on feasting, lighting candles, and gathering together for celebration through music and dance. Every culture has a winter festival. In Africa, there is the festival of the harvest, Kwanzaa. Kwanzaa celebrates family, community, and culture. The Western world has the twelve days of Christmas, and the Jewish festival of Hanukkah, the Festival of Lights. On December 8, Buddhists celebrate the Day of Enlightenment, which commemorates the day that Buddha experienced enlightenment. Many Persians celebrate the ancient ceremony of Sadeh on January 30 (fifty days before the beginning of spring), a festival of fire and light in the midst of the cold and dark. In late January or early February, Chinese New Year commences. In short, people around the world appreciate winter as a time to celebrate. The fact that winter festivals are celebrated across all cultures and historical backgrounds should be seen as common ground that allows all of us to come together to celebrate our humanity. The thread runs through many cultures and religions, joining us together in a profound way.

Decorate Your Space

Celebrating these various winter festivals gives us the opportunity to make our homes festive and full of light. During the dark days of winter, these holidays allow us to celebrate our personal histories with flair. Make the holidays uniquely yours by personalizing your decorations. Collect decorations that reflect your history and passions. Are you a sports fan? A great cook? A travel lover? An opera aficionado? Are you sentimental about the place where you live? Do you hold memories of the past dear? Do you love glamour? Are sparkly, glittery things magical for you? Think about what you and your family love most, and select the decorations that tell your own unique story.

Are you a traditionalist, an iconoclast? Are you creative and eclectic? Your passions can provide a starting point to help you decorate your home. Embrace who and what you are. Let that personality shine through in the way you set your table and adorn your home. Use the holiday season as a stage to tell your friends and family who you are and what is really important to you.

winter recipes

Erbazzone (Spinach and Cheese Tart)

I prepare this dish on Christmas Day, along with the *torta rustica*, and my family looks forward to it every year with great anticipation. It is a vitamin-packed dish of spinach, eggs, and three cheeses baked in a flaky pastry crust and cut into squares, and it is best served hot from the oven and eaten immediately.

I learned how to make *erbazzone* from my relatives in Reggio Emilia in northern Italy. If you ever visit Reggio Emilia you will find *erbazzone* everywhere—it's a staple for the Emilians—sold in small bars and neighborhood bakeries. Be careful, though: It is addictive.

SERVES 16

For the dough

1 cup (2 sticks) (226 g) salted butter, cut into small cubes

1 cup (227 g) sour cream

1 cup (142 g) all-purpose flour

For the filling

2 (10-ounce) (284 g) packages frozen spinach

¼ cup (60 ml) extra-virgin olive oil

1 onion, diced

3 cloves garlic, minced

1 cup (200 g) grated Parmigiano-Reggiano cheese

1 cup (200 g) grated Asiago cheese

1 cup (100 g) grated mozzarella cheese

4 large eggs

1 teaspoon (6 g) fine sea salt

Make the dough: Put the butter, and sour cream in a food processor. Pulse to combine and add the flour. When the dough forms a loose mass, take it out and form it into two balls. Place each ball on a sheet of lightly floured wax paper or plastic wrap and wrap tightly. Let the dough rest in the refrigerator for at least 2 hours.

Make the filling: Let the spinach thaw in a colander. Squeeze out all the water until the spinach is dry. (It is very important that there is no excess liquid in the spinach mixture.)

In a large sauté pan, heat the oil over medium-high heat. Add the onion and garlic and sauté until softened and golden brown, 5 to 7 minutes. Add the spinach and salt and sauté for 5 minutes.

Scrape the mixture into a mixing bowl and refrigerate until cool. Add cheeses and 3 of the beaten eggs and stir to combine. Set aside.

Assemble and bake the tart: Preheat the oven to 350°F (177°C) (Gas mark 4).

On a pastry cloth, using a floured rolling pin covered with a pastry stocking, roll out one ball of dough into a rectangular shape, about ⅛ inch (3 mm) thick. Transfer the dough to a baking sheet: Place a baking sheet upside down on top of the rolled-out dough, grasp the edges of the pastry cloth, and flip it over; the dough will be positioned on top of the baking sheet.

Spread the spinach mixture over the dough rectangle about 1 inch (2.5 cm) thick.

Roll out the second ball of dough into a rectangle. Using the pastry cloth to help you lift it, grasp each end and flip it over onto the filling. Turn under all the edges of the dough and crimp them closed. Beat the remaining egg in a small bowl and brush the top of the tart with the egg. Make several small cuts in the top to allow steam to escape as the tart bakes.

Bake for about 45 minutes, or until the top is golden brown and the mixture is cooked. Cut into 3-inch (7.5 cm) squares and serve on a festive platter.

Torta Rustica
(Egg, Cheese, and Prosciutto Tart)

It takes a bit of practice to get used to handling the soft pastry dough, but once you get it down it's an easy matter—and in any case this *torta* is worth every moment of beginner's frustration. It's a real treat.

SERVES 16

For the dough

1 cup (142 g) all-purpose flour

1 cup (2 sticks) (226 g) salted butter, cut into small cubes

1 cup (227 g) sour cream

For the filling

4 large eggs

1 teaspoon (6 g) sea salt

1 cup (200 g) grated Parmigiano-Reggiano cheese

1 cup (100 g) grated mozzarella cheese

1 cup (200 g) grated Asiago cheese

8 slices very thinly sliced prosciutto, preferably from Parma, Italy

Make the dough: Put the flour, butter, and sour cream in a food processor. Pulse to combine. When the dough forms a loose mass, take it out and form it into two balls. Place each ball on a sheet of lightly floured wax paper or plastic wrap and wrap tightly. Let the dough rest in the refrigerator for at least 2 hours.

Make the filling: In a large bowl, whisk 3 of the eggs just until they are liquid. Gently whisk in the salt, then fold in the grated cheeses.

Assemble and bake the tart: Preheat the oven to 350° F (177°C) (Gas mark 4).

On a pastry cloth, using a floured rolling pin covered with a pastry stocking, roll out one ball of dough into a rectangular shape, about ⅛ inch (3 mm) thick. Transfer the dough to a baking sheet: Place a baking sheet upside down on top of the rolled-out dough, grasp the edges of the pastry cloth, and flip it over; the dough will be positioned on top of the baking sheet.

Spread the cheese-egg mixture over the dough about 1 inch thick. Arrange the prosciutto slices over the top so they cover the entire cheese mixture.

Roll out the second ball of dough into a rectangle. Using the pastry cloth to help you lift it, grasp each end and flip it over onto the prosciutto. Turn under all the edges of the dough and crimp them closed. Beat the remaining egg in small bowl and brush the top of the tart with the egg. Make several small cuts in the top to allow steam to escape as the tart bakes.

Bake for about 45 minutes, or until the top is golden brown. Cut into 3-inch (7.5 cm) squares and serve on a festive platter.

Rosemary and Wild Mushroom Roasted Chicken

This delicious and well-flavored roasted chicken is a real treat on a cold, blustery night—it makes for a big, hearty meal that is very satisfying. The complex, woodsy flavor of the porcini mushrooms, together with the aromatic mixture of fresh rosemary, sage, and olive oil, make a delicious paste that is almost meat like in itself. Spreading the mixture directly on the flesh of the chicken, under the skin, infuses the bird with layers of flavors that are rich and delightful to the palate. Serve with a crisp green salad (PAGE 35) made of organic local romaine lettuce (buy a head of lettuce, not packaged leaves).

The carcass of the chicken and all the drippings from the pan should be reserved for the following evening to make the Chicken Carcass Soup (PAGE 168). Leave some meat on the bones, if you can keep midnight snackers away, to ensure a tasty and protein-rich soup.

SERVES 4

1 tablespoon (15 g) fresh rosemary needles

3 cloves garlic

1 tablespoon (18 g) sea salt

¼ cup (9 g) dried porcini mushrooms (AVAILABLE IN GOURMET GROCERY STORES), reconstituted in warm water, soaking water reserved

¼ cup (60 ml) extra-virgin olive oil

1 organic local free-range roasting chicken

1 carrot, chopped

1 rib celery with leaves, chopped

1 small onion, chopped

1 tablespoon (15 g) extra-virgin olive oil, for drizzling

very fine sea salt

Preheat the oven to 350° F (177°C) (Gas mark 4).

Mince the rosemary, garlic, salt, and reconstituted mushrooms together on a board, then drizzle with the oil and chop some more to make a thick paste.

Put the chicken in a large roasting pan and remove the giblets. Lift up the skin on the breast and push small amounts of the rosemary mixture under the skin on both sides. Make sure the mixture is well distributed all over the breast. Turn the chicken over and lift the skin on the back. Insert more of the rosemary mixture under the skin, on both sides, reserving some of the remaining mixture. Turn the chicken over and put the carrot, celery, and onion in the cavity. Drizzle with olive oil and dust with salt.

Rub the chicken all over with the remaining rosemary mixture. Bake for about 1¼ hours. Insert an instant-read meat thermometer in the crevice between the leg and the breast. There should be no pink, the juices should be clear, and the temperature should read 170° to 180° F (77° to 82°C) when the chicken is done. Move the legs; if they are loose, the chicken is done. Serve. Save the carcass and pan drippings for Rosanna's Chicken Carcass Soup (PAGE 168).

Francesca's Favorite Salad Dressing

I created this salad dressing for my daughter Francesca. I wanted to add a little interest to my usual dressing of simply olive oil, red wine vinegar, and sea salt. Here I add Dijon mustard and use balsamic vinegar, in a nod to a similar dressing I had in Paris on a particularly memorable *salade niçoise*, and then I add a smashed garlic clove to give it one more layer of flavor. This is a lovely, rich dressing that coats the leaves of the romaine lettuce in a caramel-colored sheen, and the flavor is tangy, and slightly sweet, with just a hint of garlic. The nutty, buttery quality of the olive oil and the spiciness of the mustard has me using slices of bread to soak up every drop of dressing that remains, and Francesca does the same thing every time I serve this salad. Be sure to dress the salad leaves with sea salt and freshly ground black pepper as well as the vinaigrette.

SERVES 4 AS A SIDE DISH

½ cup (120 ml) extra-virgin olive oil

1 teaspoon (5 g) Dijon mustard

Dash of balsamic vinegar, preferably Italian (such as Fini)

Sea salt to taste

1 clove garlic, smashed but left whole

1 head romaine lettuce, cut into 3-inch (7.5 cm) pieces

Put all the ingredients except the lettuce in a plastic container that has a hermetic seal. Shake the mixture vigorously until all the ingredients are blended. Open the container and discard the garlic. Toss the dressing with the lettuce and serve immediately.

Rosanna's Chicken Carcass Soup

This soup is my all-time favorite, whether for lunch or dinner—and during the winter I've been known to enjoy it twice a day. It has everything: Protein in the form of roast chicken, and veggies in the form of bright-tasting carrots and firm celery. Lastly, there are carbohydrates in the noodles that are added 15 minutes before serving. This soup is also economical: It uses deliciously seasoned leftovers—nothing is wasted. The morning after, I reheat the soup for my daughter's lunch, pouring it into a stainless-steel thermal container that fits nicely in her lunch box. The container always comes home empty. This soup is a classic and should be a part of everybody's list of favorite wintertime dishes.

Pour a nice red table wine like a Montefalco (from Umbria, Italy) or a Montepulciano (from Tuscany), and serve the soup with bread that has plenty of body and a crisp crust.

SERVES 8

2 large carrots, cut into ¼-inch-thick (6 mm) rounds

2 large ribs celery, cut into 2-inch (5 cm) lengths

Carcass and pan drippings from a roasted chicken (PAGE 167)

1 pound (454 g) dried pappardelle (wide egg noodles, preferably De Cecco brand)

Fill a large soup pot halfway with water. Add the carrots, celery, and chicken carcass and pan drippings. Bring to a boil over high heat. Boil for about 5 minutes, then remove the carcass and pull off any meat with a fork and return the meat to the pot. Cook over low heat for about 1 hour. Just before serving, add the pasta. Gently break the nests of noodles so they aren't too long. Cook at a simmer for about 15 minutes, until the noodles are soft and thoroughly cooked. Serve hot, in low, shallow bowls about 8 inches in diameter. Light candles and play some Pavarotti while dining. Make sure to save some for your child's lunchbox!

Simple Risotto

Risotto is an Italian rice dish from the north of Italy near Milan. With *osso bucco* (SEE RECIPE ON PAGE 171), *risotto alla Milanese* is usually served, but I prefer to serve a simple version of risotto without saffron, letting the flavors of a dry white wine take its place. *Osso bucco* is so complex and delicious itself that I don't want the saffron flavor to compete with the meat.

When you make risotto, you must stay at the stove and add ladlefuls of hot chicken broth, one at a time, letting each become absorbed before adding the next, until the rice is creamy and the grains are soft. I add the wine in the middle of the process, as I prefer the wine to cook off and leave just a hint of its flavor. I spoon the risotto into low-rimmed individual soup bowls and then top each serving with a single veal shank. This dish is very satisfying and has wonderfully complex combinations of flavors and textures. When you and your guests eat, there will be silence at the table—a sure sign that you've succeeded in the kitchen.

SERVES 4

½ cup (1 stick) (113 g) butter

¼ cup (60 ml) extra-virgin olive oil

½ yellow onion, chopped

2 cups (360 g) Italian Aborio rice

1 quart (1 liter) organic chicken broth, heated on stove

1 cup (250 ml) dry white wine

In a large, heavy-bottomed sauté pan, melt the butter over medium heat. Add the oil and onion and sauté until the onion is soft, 5 to 7 minutes.

Add the rice and cook for about 1 minute, stirring to coat all the rice grains with the butter and oil. Add a ladleful of the heated broth and cook at a simmer, stirring frequently, until the rice has absorbed almost all of the broth. Add another ladleful of broth and continue to cook until half of the broth is absorbed. Add the wine and simmer for about 5 minutes, then slowly add the rest of the broth. Cook until the risotto is milky and creamy and the grains of rice are soft but still hold their shape. Scoop the risotto onto serving plates and top with the *osso bucco* (PAGE 171), if you'd like, drizzled with juices from the veal. Let the dish sit about 10 minutes before serving.

Osso Bucco (Braised Veal Shanks)

Osso bucco means "bone with a hole" in Italian, and refers to a cross-cut of veal shank that's about 3 inches (7.5 cm) thick. In most shops it's considered a specialty cut, so you might need to ask your butcher to order it ahead of time, especially during the holidays.

I serve this dish every Christmas Eve. It is delicious, imbued with hints of white wine, beef broth, and a variety of herbs. Slowly cooked for many hours, the meat becomes extremely tender, literally melting in your mouth, and has so many notes of flavor that the experience of eating it is unforgettable. I serve the shanks on a mound of simple risotto (SEE RECIPE ON PAGE 169) and top off the presentation with sauce from the pan and a sprinkling of minced parsley, grated lemon zest, and chopped garlic. It is best to let the meat rest for about 10 minutes on the plates before serving, as the braised meat and the risotto are both extremely hot and can burn eager tongues.

Don't overlook the best part of the dish: the bone marrow. Scoop it out from the center of the bone with an espresso spoon. It is heavenly—a wonderful custard consistency that is imbued with all the flavors of the herbs, wine, and broth.

SERVES 4

½ cup (120 ml) extra-virgin olive oil

½ cup (1 stick) (113 g) butter

¾ cup (108 g) all-purpose flour

Sea salt and freshly ground black pepper

4 veal shanks, about 3 inches (7.5 cm) thick, tied around the circumference with twine

1 large yellow onion, finely chopped

3 ribs celery with leaves, finely chopped

3 carrots, finely chopped

1 cup (250 ml) dry white wine

1 to 2 cups (250 to 500 ml) beef broth

¼ cup (60 g) chopped canned San Marzano tomatoes, or ¼ cup (60 g) Rosanna's Tomato Sauce (PAGE 172)

½ teaspoon (2.5 g) dried thyme

½ teaspoon (2.5 g) dried marjoram

6 fresh basil leaves

2 bay leaves

½ cup (80 g) chopped fresh flat-leaf parsley

3 strips lemon zest

3 cloves garlic

Preheat the oven to 250° F (121°C) (Gas mark ½).

Put the oil and butter in a large, low casserole at least 12 inches (30.5 cm) in circumference and 4 inches (10 cm) deep and place over medium heat. Season the flour with salt and pepper to taste, then dredge the meat in the flour, shaking off any excess. Add the meat to the casserole and cook, turning, until golden brown on all sides, about 20 minutes total. Remove the meat to a platter. Add the onion, celery, and carrots and cook until the onion is translucent, about 5 minutes.

Deglaze the pan with the wine, scraping up all the browned bits from the pan so they become part of the sauce. Add 1 ½ cups (375 ml) of the broth, the tomatoes, thyme, marjoram, basil, bay leaves, and salt and pepper to taste. Bring to a boil. Return the meat to the casserole. Make sure the meat is mostly covered with the broth; just the tops of the shanks should be visible. If not, add more broth. Cover the casserole and transfer to the oven. Bake for 5 hours, adding more broth if the mixture becomes too dry, until the meat is extremely tender. Finely mince the parsley, lemon zest, and garlic together on a board, then sprinkle the mixture over the meat. Serve, with espresso spoons for scooping out the marrow, on top of Simple Risotto (PAGE 169).

Rosanna's Tomato Sauce

My friends tell me this is my signature dish. My extended family always asks me to make it for every occasion we are together. I have given containers of this sauce to friends after a dinner party as a memento of the time we spent together at my table. This sauce is also my best-kept secret for quick meals after a long day at work and for surprise guests who pop in to visit. I make huge batches of this sauce on a Sunday and cool it in the refrigerator. I have plastic freezer containers ready to be filled with three ladles each of this delicious sauce to be frozen for those times I just don't feel like cooking.

If you want to have enough to freeze, double the recipe. Then, whenever you want a quick dinner, just take out a container and heat it up (along with a little water).

This sauce, whether frozen and thawed or freshly made, can also serve as a base for many other sauces. It can be used with any pasta, but my favorite shapes are penne *rigate*, linguine *fini* (fine linguine), pappardelle, spaghetti *alla chitarra* (spaghetti cut on a guitar string), and curly campanelle. My favorite brand is De Cecco, but I also like Barilla and some of the artisan pasta that Williams-Sonoma carries in its gourmet food section.

Pasta can be a complete meal, with a lovely salad and a nice glass of wine. And there's no need to serve bread: In Italy you never eat two starches together. This sauce will make your life so easy. If you try it, you'll love it!

The sauce is wonderful as is, but if you want something fancier, try the divine vodka cream sauce variation on page 89.

MAKES 6 SERVINGS

1 large carrot

2 ribs celery with leaves

1 onion

4 cloves garlic

½ cup (120 ml) good-quality extra-virgin olive oil

2 (28-ounce) (794 g) cans San Marzano tomatoes

1 teaspoon (6 g) sea salt

½ teaspoon (3 g) sugar (if necessary)

Chop the carrot, celery, onion, and garlic (this can also be done in a food processor).

Put the oil in a large saucepan and place over medium heat. When the oil is hot, add the chopped vegetables and sauté over medium heat until just soft, about 5 minutes.

Puree the tomatoes in a food processor, then add them to the pan. Add the salt and sugar if necessary (I find that the San Marzano tomatoes are usually sweet enough on their own). Let the sauce simmer, uncovered, for 1 hour, stirring occasionally.

That's the basic recipe, but I believe the best way to make this sauce is to cook by feel. Just go by what smells and tastes right to you. *Buon appetito!*

Gingerbread

One of my first memories as a small child is of Mother's homemade gingerbread. I would walk through the door after school and smell the intoxicating mix of spices that filled the kitchen with the comforting aroma of a homemade dessert. My mother always timed it so the gingerbread was still warm when I got home and served it with a big spoonful of whipped cream on the side. I loved the combination of the spicy, exotic ginger cake with the velvety smooth whipped cream made with country-fresh cream from a nearby dairy. The cake and the cream together made my toes tingle and sent shivers up my spine, and now, so many years later, it has become true comfort food for me. Try this on a cold, blustery night. You will understand how to start making memories with food.

SERVES 6

2½ cups (355 g) all-purpose flour

1 teaspoon (.9 g) ground cinnamon

2 teaspoons (1.2 g) ground ginger

1 teaspoon (.9 g) ground cloves

½ cup (1 stick) (113 g) butter, softened

½ cup (100 g) sugar

1 cup (340 g) dark molasses

1 tablespoon (21 g) honey (optional)

1 teaspoon (1.8 g) baking soda

1 cup (250 ml) boiling water

2 large eggs, lightly beaten

Whipped cream, for serving

Preheat the oven to 350° F (177°C) (Gas mark 4). Grease and lightly flour an 8-inch (20 cm) square pan.

Sift together the flour, cinnamon, ginger, and cloves onto a piece of wax paper.

Put the butter in a large mixing bowl and beat until it is smooth and creamy. Blend in the sugar, molasses, and honey if using.

In a small bowl, stir together the baking soda and boiling water, then pour into the butter mixture, beating well. Add the flour mixture and continue to beat until the batter is smooth. Beat in the eggs.

Pour the batter into the prepared pan and bake for 45 to 55 minutes, until a toothpick inserted in the center of the cake comes out clean. Remove from the oven and let cool in the pan for 5 minutes, then turn out onto a rack. Serve warm or at room temperature with whipped cream.

My Mother's Sugar Cookies

My mother made dozens upon dozens of cookies for Christmas every year. She would begin her baking spree about two weeks before the holiday and finish on the day before Christmas Eve. Sometimes she was nervous, and we were banned from the kitchen so she could devote her full attention to the task of baking: Her recipes were precious and she was a perfectionist, and we could not be bothering her when she was in the thick of preparing some of the more complex recipes. However, the sugar cookies were all ours. She allowed us to roll them out, cut them in shapes to our fancy, and sprinkle them with a wide variety of sparkly sugar confections. They were always delicate and crunchy. "The secret to delicious pastry is to not overwork the dough, girls," she would say. I remember her words to this day, and I repeat them to my girls, who I hope will repeat them to their girls, and so on . . .

These are wonderful cookies to be enjoyed in the making and the eating, and a wonderful tradition to start with loved ones.

MAKES ABOUT 24 COOKIES

2 cups (284 g) all-purpose flour

½ teaspoon (.9 g) baking soda

¼ teaspoon (1.5 g) salt

½ cup (1 stick) (113 g) butter, softened

1 cup (200 g) sugar

1 large egg

1 tablespoon (15 ml) vanilla extract

Colored sugar crystals or candy sprinkles

Sift together the flour, baking soda, and salt onto a piece of wax paper. Set aside.

Using an electric mixer, cream the butter and sugar. Add the egg and vanilla and beat well. Add the dry ingredients a little at a time and mix until well combined. Wrap the dough in a clean kitchen towel or parchment paper and chill in the refrigerator for at least 30 minutes.

Preheat the oven to 400°F (204°C) (Gas mark 6). Butter baking sheets.

Roll out one-third of the dough to about ⅛ inch (3 mm) thick and cut out shapes with cookie cutters. Sprinkle the cookies generously with colored sugar crystals or candy sprinkles and transfer the shapes to the prepared baking sheets. Bake for 10 minutes, or until firm in the centers but not browned. Remove the cookies from the sheets with a wide spatula and cool on wire racks. Repeat with the remaining dough. Store the cookies in a tin. They can be frozen prior to the holiday for up to 1 month, or stored in a cool, dark place for 1 week.

Michael's Cookies

MAKES ABOUT 1 DOZEN COOKIES

Named after my nephew, who cannot get enough of them, these delicious cookies are sandwiched with a luscious mocha filling and dipped in semisweet chocolate and nuts.

For the cookies

1 cup (2 sticks) (226 g) unsalted butter

½ cup (56 g) confectioners' sugar

½ teaspoon (2.5 ml) vanilla extract

2 cups (284 g) all-purpose flour

¼ teaspoon (1.5 g) baking powder

For the filling

²/₃ cup (76 g) confectioners' sugar

2 tablespoons (28 g) unsalted butter, softened

1 tablespoon (15 ml) brewed espresso

A little milk if necessary

For the coating

1 (12-ounce) (340 g) bag semisweet chocolate ships, melted and kept warm

1 cup (340 g) chopped toasted pecans

Make the cookies: Preheat the oven to 375°F (191°C) (Gas mark 5)

In a large bowl, using an electric mixer, cream the butter. Continuing to beat, add the confectioners' sugar and vanilla, then the flour and baking powder. Using a cookie press with a medium star pattern, press out 3-inch fingers onto the prepared baking sheet, keeping them as straight as possible because they will be joined together with filling later. If the dough is too stiff and difficult to extrude, let it sit at room temperature until softened, if necessary. Bake for about 7 minutes, until firm but not browned. Let the cookies cool, then move carefully to a wire rack. They will be very delicate.

Make the filling: Beat all the ingredients together to make a smooth and spreadable frosting, adding milk if necessary.

Spread the filling on the flat side of one cookie, top with the flat side of another cookie, and set it on the baking sheet and continue to make sandwiches of all the cookies.

Coat the cookies: Dip each end of each sandwich in the melted chocolate, then in the nuts. Let sit on the baking sheet until the chocolate is hardened. Store the cookies in a tin, with the layers separated by wax paper. They will keep in a tin for about 1 week or can be frozen for 2 to 3 weeks.

Rosanna's Hot Toddies

I make these hot toddies to enjoy while we decorate the tree. They are very simple to prepare and warm the body as well as the heart when the festivities are taking place. Make sure to use good-quality lemons and oranges; they make a difference in the flavor of the toddy. The oranges should be sweet and juicy.

I prefer Cognac, but brandy, rum, or Irish whiskey would be delicious, too. For children's toddies, simply omit the liquor and add an extra slice of orange.

SERVES 1

3 strips lemon zest

1 slice of orange

1 sprinkle of cinnamon

1 sprinkle of freshly grated nutmeg

1 tablespoon (21 g) local honey

1 jigger Cognac

Boiling water

Muddle all the ingredients except the water in an oversized porcelain Rosanna holiday mug. Fill with boiling water and let steep for a few minutes.

Sip while decorating your home. Light candles, put on some Placido Domingo holiday music, and relax.

Rosanna's Mocha

Although I have traveled throughout Italy extensively and have a deep appreciation for fine espresso made in the old style, I still love a good cup of Starbucks coffee. My favorite coffees from Starbucks are Sumatra and the Italian Roast—the former works best here. I love this mocha because it's low in fat and has just a hint of chocolate. I treat my daughter and myself to this drink after a meal as a dessert instead of eating something heavy. It also serves as a great pick-me-up during the day when you don't want too much coffee.

whole beans

2% milk

1 teaspoon (7 g) honey

1 teaspoon (7 g) Starbucks mocha powder

¼ cup (63 ml) or 1 shot espresso

Mocha or sweetened cocoa powder

Grind whole beans to a very fine grind and make espresso. Heat 2% milk in a small saucepan until it steams but does not boil. In a Rosanna porcelain mug, combine 1 teaspoon (7 g) honey and 1 teaspoon (5 g) Starbucks mocha powder and pour in the heated milk, stirring to combine. Add about ¼ cup (63 ml) or 1 shot of espresso, stir, and top it off with a sprinkle of mocha or sweetened cocoa powder. Play Frank Sinatra or Ella Fitzgerald holiday jazz.

Celestial Seasonings Chamomile Tea

I love Celestial Seasonings. The herbal-tea company was created by hippies in the '70s, and there is something spiritual and inherently good about their teas. The packages always tell a story, and I trust their product. I particularly love their chamomile tea. I am a two-bagger, because I need the extra bag to totally relax me. I don't usually sweeten my tea, but this one is lovely with a small espresso-size spoonful of local honey if you like a touch of sweetness. The tea relaxes me naturally; sometimes I have it after work, sometimes just before I go to bed. It's a must for unwinding.

Boil water. Put 2 tea bags in a large porcelain mug, add the boiling water, and let steep for a few minutes. Sip slowly, light some candles, and relax with some great jazz. (Try Chet Baker or Astrud Gilberto.)

Taylors of Harrogate

I love everything British, but this is one of my favorite tea companies. Taylors of Harrogate black teas—such as English Breakfast, Afternoon Darjeeling, Pure Ceylon, or, my favorite, Yorkshire Tea—are dark, rich, and extremely satisfying. I do not steep them for the recommended time, but only for about 3 minutes, or about 20 dunks of the tea bag, because I don't like my tea too strong. If you like darker tea, leave the bag or tea ball in the water for a bit longer. I take these teas with milk, and they're also delicious with local honey for a little sweetness.

Celestial Seasonings Peppermint Tea

I love this tea either just before bed or after a substantial meal. It is a quieting tea that to me seems to foster sweet dreams, and a good homeopathic remedy for an upset tummy. There's no need for sweetener, as the lovely peppermint seems to taste a little sweet on its own.

Place 1 tea bag in a friendly shaped porcelain mug and pour boiling water over it. Play the soundtrack from *The Painted Veil*, then drift off to sleep with a settled stomach and the refreshing scent of peppermint in the air.

Yorkshire Tea

Sold by the British tea merchant Taylors of Harrogate, Yorkshire Tea is a wonderfully rich black tea blended to exacting standards—they even make a version specially blended for hard water!

Place 1 tea bag in a large porcelain mug. Bring water almost to a boil and pour it over the tea bag. Let steep, but not too long—I prefer a lighter tea with not too much tannin. Play the soundtrack from *Love Actually* or *Pride & Prejudice*.

Hot Water in a Mug

This is a great drink to enjoy while you're cooking dinner. It suppresses your appetite to help you feel full until dinner's ready. (Play Vince Guaraldi's *A Charlie Brown Christmas,* a lighthearted and festive jazz composition, perfect for the holidays, while you cook.) Also, try drinking hot water during the day instead of flavored drinks. It's good for your body and keeps you warm. Be sure to use a pretty porcelain mug, which makes even plain water feel special.

acknowledgments

My deepest thanks to my dear friend and agent, Dr. Pepper Schwartz, who has supported me professionally and personally for over 25 years. Your friendship gives me strength and joy.

A grateful thank you to my wonderful photographer, John Granen, who has captured my homes and family so beautifully for this book and numerous publications. John, you truly have the eye of an artist. Thank you for capturing my vision of the world on film.

Jennifer Levesque, my editor, how can I thank you enough? Your patience and support have been invaluable. Your early belief in the book helped me communicate my message of coming together as a multi-generational family. A special thank you to my assistant, Michelle Jensen, who met my every request with professionalism and enthusiasm.

The support I have received from everyone at Rosanna, Inc. has given me the energy and belief in myself to write this book. Thank you to a wonderful staff. My gratitude to Alessandra, my clever daughter, who lent me her writing expertise to help create this book. To my dear women friends Drindy, Tammy, and Deby, who supported me in the most profound way while I was writing this book. Thanks to my sister Vicki who is one of most hard-working women I know: you continue the traditions that our Mother taught us. Your dedication to family is a tribute to our parents. To Mimmo, as I have said to you many years ago, the eyes are the mirror of the soul; thank you for opening my eyes to the beauty of romance. Alessandra and Francesca, you make my life worth living.

Last but certainly not least, I thank my dear family who posed for countless photo shoots, ate copious amounts of food when I was testing recipes, and cheered me on throughout the entire process. You are so dear to me. I think of this book as a labor of love dedicated to you, my family, my life. You are where everything good begins. You are home.

index

A

After-school wild blackberry pie, 134
Antiques, appreciation of, 64-66
Apple dumplings, my mother's, 132
Artichokes, 34
Asparagus
    with fried eggs, 32
    frittata, 33
    in the oven, 32
Atmosphere, creating, 155

B

Back to school, 101-103
    college, 104-105
Bag lunches, 111
Beverages
    caffè scherato, 97
    chamomile tea, 177
    hot water in a mug, 178
    iced caffè latte, 97
    peppermint tea, 178
    Rosanna's hot toddies, 177
    Rosanna's mocha, 177
    Yorkshire tea, 178
Birthday party, spring, 19
Biscuits, and sugar butter, Pat's, 46
Blackberry pie, after-school, 134
Burn-your-fingers lamb, 94
Butterscotch pie, 42

C

Caffè latte, iced, 97
Caffè scherato, 97
Cakes
    Cindy's bunny, 45
    Grandma's caramel, 139
California brown rice, 34
Caramel cake, Grandma's, 139
Celestial Seasonings, 177, 178
Chamomile tea, Celestial Seasonings, 177
Chicken, rosemary and wild mushroom
    roasted, 167
Childhood, prolonging, 107
Chocolate chip pancakes, sleepover, 48
Christmas, recipes for, 164, 171
Cindy's bunny cake, 45

Cinnamon crust, 138
Coconut cream pie, 43
Cookies
    Michael's, 176
    my mother's sugar, 174
    owl, 140
Cultures, blending of, 78-80
Cupcake frosting, Rosanna's quick, 143
Cupcakes, 49
    pumpkin and cat, 143

D

Dance, to celebrate spring, 22
Daniela and Vito's out-of-this-world
    pizza toppings, 88
Decorating
    for spring, 25-26
    for winter, 161

E

Egg, cheese, and prosciutto tart, 166
Erbazzone, 164

F

Fall, 101
    field trips for, 109
    going to college, 104-105
    Halloween, 114-121
    harvest festivals, 122
    natural transformations in, 113
    postponing feeling of, 102-108
    recipes for, 126-143
    Thanksgiving, 122-123
Family history, appreciation of, 64-66
France, lifestyle of, 101
Francesca's favorite salad dressing, 168
Frittata di asparagi, 33

G

Games, outdoor, 21
Gingerbread, 173
Giving, importance of, 156
Golden harvest peach pie, 137
Grandma's caramel cake, 139
Gravy, turkey, 128

Greengrocer-style pasta, 36

H

Halloween, 114-121
    recipes for, 128
Hamburgers alla Italiana, 88-89
Harvest festivals, 122
Hearing, sense of, 62-63
Homemade popcorn in the pan, 49
Homemaking, value of, 156-157
Hot toddies, Rosanna's, 177
Hot water in a mug, 178

I

Iced caffè latte, 97
Insalata
    estiva, 90
    mista, 35
Introspection, value of, 158
Italy, lifestyle of, 54-84
Ivana's pasta alla Norcina, 92

L

Lamb, burn-your-fingers, 94
Lentil soup, Rosanna's, 131

M

May Day, 27-28
Memories, making, 151
Michael's cookies, 176
Mixed salad, 35
Mocha, Rosanna's, 177
Movie night with the girls, 106
My mom's extra flaky pie crust dough, 138
My mother's apple dumplings, 132
My mother's sugar cookies, 174

N

Nostalgia, 151

O

Osso bucco, 171
Outdoor games, 21

Oven-roasted Halloween pumpkin seeds, 128
Owl cookies, 140

P

Paglia e fieno, 38
Pancakes, sleepover chocolate chip, 48
Pantry, contents of, 68-69
Party
    planning, 20
    spring birthday, 19
Pasta
    estiva, 91
    greengrocer-style, 36
    alla Norcina, 92
    straw and hay, 38
    tomato-vodka, 89-90
Pat's biscuits and sugar butter, 46
Peppermint tea, Celestial Seasonings, 178
Physical activity, to celebrate spring, 18
Pie crust dough, my mom's extra flaky, 138
Pies
    after-school wild blackberry, 134
    butterscotch, 42
    coconut cream, 43
    golden harvest peach, 137
    ricotta tart, 96
Pizza, 74
    toppings for, 88
Popcorn, homemade in the pan, 49
Pork
    chops with extra-virgin olive oil and fresh herbs, 94
    loin chops, 39
    rib roast with fresh herbs and sea salt, 41
Potato wedges, roasted, with olive oil and oregano, 129
Potatoes, small roasted red, 35
Pranzo, 84
Pumpkin and cat cupcakes, 143
Pumpkins, carving, 115
Restaurant, becoming a regular at, 75-77

R

Rice, California brown, 34
Ricotta tart, 96
Risotto, simple, 169
Roasted potato wedges with olive oil and oregano, 129

Rosanna's chicken carcass soup, 168
Rosanna's hot toddies, 177
Rosanna's lentil soup, 131
Rosanna's mocha, 177
Rosanna's quick cupcake frosting, 143
Rosanna's Thanksgiving turkey, 126
Rosanna's tomato sauce, 172
Rosanna's tomato-vodka pasta sauce, 89-90
Rosemary and wild mushroom roasted chicken, 167

S

Salad dressing, Francesca's favorite, 168
Salads
    mixed, 35
    summer, 90
Salmon, wild Alaska sockeye, 41
Scottadito d'agnello, 94
Shakerato, 97
Sight, sense of, 57
Simple risotto, 169
Sleepover chocolate chip pancakes, 48
Small roasted red potatoes, 35
Smell, sense of, 58
Soups
    Rosanna's chicken carcass, 168
    Rosanna's lentil, 131
Souvenirs, 83
Spinach and cheese tart, 164
Spinach soufflé, 131
Sports, 112-113
Spring, 11
    birthday party, 19
    celebrating, 12, 15, 21
    decorating for, 25-26
    holidays in, 27-28
    and physical activity, 18
    recipes for, 32-49
    vegetables of, 16
Spring break, 28
    plan for, 29
Spring cleaning, 23
    plan for, 24
Squash, Thanksgiving, 128
Straw and hay pasta, 38
Sugar butter, 46
Sugar cookies, my mother's, 174

Summer
    entertaining in, 70-73
    experiencing, 56-63
    foods of, 66-67
    neighborhoods in, 53-54
    recipes of, 88-97
    vegetables of, 58
Summer pasta, 91
Summer salad, 90

T

Taste, sense of, 58
Taylors of Harrogate, 178
Thanksgiving, 122-123
    recipes for, 126-129
Timballo di spinaci, 131
Time, passage of, 113
Tomato sauce, Rosanna's, 172
Tomato-vodka pasta sauce, 89-90
Torta rustica, 166
Touch, sense of, 61
Turkey
    gravy for, 128
    Rosanna's Thanksgiving, 126

V

Veal shanks, braised, 171
Vegetables
    spring, 16
    Thanksgiving roasted, 129

W

Water, hot, in a mug, 178
Wild Alaska sockeye salmon, 41
Winter
    comfort in, 152-153
    decorating for, 161
    festivals of, 160
    memories of, 151
    recipes for, 164-178
    traditions of, 147-150

Y

Yorkshire tea, 178